A Teacher's Guide to
Mentor Texts

ALLISON MARCHETTI • REBEKAH O'DELL

A Teacher's Guide to

Mentor Texts

GRADES 6–12

Series Editor Katie Wood Ray

HEINEMANN
PORTSMOUTH, NH

Heinemann

145 Maplewood Avenue, Suite 300

Portsmouth, NH 03801

www.heinemann.com

Offices and agents throughout the world

© 2021 by Allison Marchetti and Rebekah O'Dell

The authors and publisher wish to thank those who have generously given permission to reprint borrowed material:

"October Heart" and "Autobiography" illustrated by Mari Andrew. Copyright © by Mari Andrew. Reprinted by permission of the illustrator.

Drowned City: Hurricane Katrina and New Orleans by Don Brown. Copyright © 2015 by Don Brown. Reprinted by permission of Houghton Mifflin Harcourt Publishing Company. All rights reserved.

The Unwanted: Stories of the Syrian Refugees by Don Brown. Copyright © 2015 by Don Brown. Reprinted by permission of Houghton Mifflin Harcourt Publishing Company. All rights reserved.

"Something You Should Know" from *Counting Decent* by Clint Smith. Copyright © 2016 by Write Bloody Publishing. Published by Write Bloody Publishing. Reprinted by permission of publisher.

Text from Kwame Alexander author biography. Copyright © by Kwame Alexander. Reprinted by permission of the author.

Tracie Baptiste's author biography from *The Jumbies* by Tracie Baptiste. Copyright © 2015 by Algonquin Young Readers. Reprinted by permission of the publisher.

Jason Reynolds' author biography from *Long Way Down* by Jason Reynolds. Text copyright © 2017 by Jason Reynolds. Reprinted with the permission of Atheneum Books for Young Readers, an imprint of Simon & Schuster Children's Publishing Division. All rights reserved.

Text from "'The Lion King' Had the Perfect Villain Song. This Time, 'Be Prepared' for Less" by Glen Weldon, originally published on npr.org on July 17, 2019. Copyright © 2019 by National Public Radio, Inc. Reprinted by permission of NPR. Any unauthorized duplication is strictly prohibited.

Text from "What Martin Luther King Jr. Taught Us About Embracing Our Enemies" by Eboo Patel, originally published in *Chicago Tribune.* Copyright © 2021 by *Chicago Tribune.* All rights reserved. Reprinted by permission of the publisher.

Text from "Auschwitz was Liberated 75 years ago. But the Holocaust is still closer than you think" by Leonard Pitts Jr., originally published in the *Miami Herald.* Copyright © 2020 by McClatchy. All rights reserved. Used under license.

Text from "Harry Potter and the Poorly-Read Exorcists" by Margaret Renkl, originally published in *The New York Times.* Copyright © 2019 by The New York Times Company. All rights reserved. Used under license.

Excerpt(s) from *Behind the Beautiful Forevers: Life, Death, and Hope in a Mumbai Under City* by Katherine Boo. Copyright © 2012 by Katherine Boo. Used by permission of Random House, an imprint and division of Penguin Random House LLC. All rights reserved.

Excerpt(s) from *It's What I Do: A Photographer's Life of Love and War* by Lynsey Addario. Copyright © 2015 by Lynsey Addario. Used by permission of Penguin Press, an imprint of Penguin Publishing Group, a division of Penguin Random House LLC. All rights reserved.

Excerpt(s) from *Lab Girl* by Hope Jahren. Copyright © 2016 by A. Hope Jahren. Used by permission of Alfred A. Knopf, an imprint of the Knopf Doubleday Publishing Group, a division of Penguin Random House LLC. All rights reserved.

Interior photographs: page 13 © Seventy-four Images / Alamy Stock Photo; page 46 © SDI Productions / Getty Images; page 51 © Ian Shaw / Alamy Stock Photo; page 53 © Jacob Lund / Alamy Stock Photo; page 67 © Erickson Stock / Alamy Stock Photo; page 71 © lovro77 / Getty Images; page 73 © Hill Street Studios / Getty Images; page 75 © SDI Productions / Getty Images; textured backgrounds used throughout, © Apostrophe / Shutterstock / HIP; watercolor art used throughout, © White Snow / Shutterstock

Library of Congress Cataloging-in-Publication Data

Names: Marchetti, Allison, author. | O'Dell, Rebekah, author.

Title: A teacher's guide to mentor texts / Allison Marchetti and Rebekah O'Dell.

Description: Portsmouth, NH : Heinemann Publishing, 2021. | Series: Classroom essentials | Includes bibliographical references.

Identifiers: LCCN 2020047096 | ISBN 9780325120034

Subjects: LCSH: English language—Composition and exercises—Study and teaching (Secondary) | Mentor texts (Language arts).

Classification: LCC LB1631 .M385477 2021 | DDC 428.0071/2—dc23

LC record available at https://lccn.loc.gov/2020047096

Editors: Katie Wood Ray and Holly Kim Price

Production: Sean Moreau

Videography: Sherry Day, Joanne Smith, and Paul Tomasyan

Cover and interior designs, typesetting: Vita Lane

Manufacturing: Val Cooper

Printed in the United States of America on acid-free paper

2 3 4 5 CGB 25 24 23 22 21

September 2021 Printing

For KWR,
our true guide.

BOOK MAP

CHAPTER FOUR

55 Learning About Structure

CHAPTER FIVE

77 Learning About Genre

About the Online Resources in This Book

The Online Resources for *A Teacher's Guide to Mentor Texts* include a variety of helpful forms and documents for you to utilize with your students as they work with mentor texts.

ONLINE RESOURCE 2–1
Five supports for reading like writers

ONLINE RESOURCE 3–1
Blank chart for craft study across the week

ONLINE RESOURCE 3–2
All the mentor text examples from the book, plus more, organized and ready for you to use in your own classroom

ONLINE RESOURCE 3–3
A blank notebook chart for craft study

ONLINE RESOURCE 3–4
Student directions for making craft lookbooks

ONLINE RESOURCE 4–1
A complete text annotated for structure

ONLINE RESOURCE 4–2
A blank teacher's craftbook for you to collect and organize your own mentor text examples

ONLINE RESOURCE 6–1A–C
All you need for a genre study of op-ed writing in your classroom: three complete texts, with and without craft annotations, and a blank chart for recording musts and mights

ONLINE RESOURCE 6–2
A helpful template for planning a whole unit with mentor texts

ONLINE RESOURCE 6–3
A helpful template for planning an instruction lesson with mentor texts

Look for this arrow throughout the book for Online Resources that can be downloaded. See page xi for instructions on how to access the Online Resources.

Additionally, you will find seventeen videos clips of Allison and Rebekah teaching with mentor texts.

How to Access the Online Resources and Videos

To access the Online Resources for *A Teacher's Guide to Mentor Texts*:

1. Go to **http://hein.pub/MentorTexts-login.**

2. Log in with your username and password. If you do not already have an account with Heinemann, you will need to create an account.

3. On the Welcome page, choose **"Click here to register an Online Resource."**

4. Register your product by entering the code **MENTORTEXT** (be sure to read and check the acknowledgment box under the keycode).

5. Once you have registered your product, it will appear alphabetically in your account list of **My Online Resources.**

Note: When returning to Heinemann.com to access your previously registered products, simply log into your Heinemann account and click on **"View my registered Online Resources."**

chapter one

WHY Mentor Texts?

sets up a question-and-answer structure

W elcome, writing teacher friend! We're guessing you're here because you want to help your students become stronger writers, and here's the guarantee we can confidently make: studying mentor texts will elevate your students' writing. In these pages, we're going to show you how, but before we get going, let's try a little mentor-text study ourselves with Mari Andrew's "October Heart."

In this text, Andrew is exploring what is in her heart one October. Look closely. What do you notice? What strikes you about the visual elements—color, shape, texture? What about word choice—do you notice any patterns?

Using her heart as a guide, think about what's in your heart for your student writers *right now*. What comes to mind when you think of them? What do you wonder about? What are your dreamiest dreams for them?

Now, try making a writing-teacher heart. Combine what you noticed about Andrew's "October Heart" with the hopes for your student writers. There's no right or wrong way to do this—just grab some inspiration and try it!

"October Heart"
by Mari Andrew

That's it! You just engaged in the whole process of mentor-text study. Very simply, a mentor text is a text created by a professional that helps us make texts of our own. And all those wishes for your student writers? Well, no matter how you teach writing, the right mentor texts can help make those wishes a reality. We can't teach genius, but we can teach students to study mentor texts and use them to produce excellent writing of their own.

Mentor texts teach writers how to

- discover, expand, and develop ideas,
- structure a piece of writing,
- organize their thoughts, and
- craft their texts to match their intentions.

SPOTLIGHT ON
STUDENT WORK

After studying this article . . .

. . . with writing in it like this . . .

10 Times Aretha Franklin Improved on Other People's Songs

by Milo Davidson, *Vulture* (August 16, 2018)

What does joy sound like? This. Just don't listen to the lyrics of this questionably intentioned Stephen Stills song, "And if you can't be with the one you love, honey / Love the one you're with." Singing a song about settling, Aretha Franklin manages to exude pure happiness and love of the world—transforming what is at best a "huh?" moment into an ode to contentment and finding triumph within yourself.

Uses the structure of a listicle, analyzing one song at a time.

"Homecoming" by Kanye West

Kanye West creates a scene in this song as if someone is proudly marching back into their home. This is another song with a piano, but the notes are lower and faster, causing the listener to feel more confident. Chris Martin sings the chorus in this song, and the lyrics remind me of what Odysseus would say; he's wondering if Penelope is thinking about him, and he wants to restart his life with her. I can see how Odysseus would want to restart his life when the book says, "The suitors shouted, and Athena stood beside Odysseus, and prompted him to go among the suitors, begging scraps. . . . He went around and begged from left to right, holding his hand out, like a practical beggar" (398). This shows how long Odysseus has been gone because he has to beg in his own house.

Begins with what the song sounds like.

Starts with the what (a description or synopsis of the song) and then explains the why (why this song is included in the list).

Writes about songs and texts in emotional terms.

Qualities of Mentor Texts

You will see mentor-text possibilities everywhere, but good mentor texts—the kind that will help your student writers grow—aren't just *any* pieces of professional writing.

Mentor Texts Are Engaging and Relevant

To impact student writing, the ideas in mentor texts need to engage the writers sitting in our classrooms *right now*. And that changes. Some years we have students who are into basketball; other years it's anime or K-pop. Sometimes, particularly in the case of op-eds or pop culture analysis, this means that mentor texts are hot off the press. In more timeless genres like poetry or fiction, mentor texts still need to be relevant by addressing the interests of the writers we are aiming to guide.

Mentor Texts Are Professionally Crafted

Mentor texts are crafted by professionals and aspirational by design, so they need to have the kind of writing that makes you want to grab a highlighter, read it out loud to no one in particular, and text your English-teacher best friend. If a text doesn't make you excited as a reader, it's probably not the right text to inspire your student writers. And while very few students will actually produce writing on par with the pros, we want every student in the room to believe that level of writing is achievable.

> " We read with the very real understanding that a great mentor text may be waiting just a page-turn away. We read with a sense of possibility because everything we teach is grounded in the writing we love. "
>
> —Allison Marchetti and Rebekah O'Dell,
> *Writing with Mentors* (2015, 14)

Mentor Texts Inspire and Guide

Reading the work of a mentor exposes student writers to new genres, new ideas, and new ways of using language. You'll know you're looking at a potential mentor text if ideas for your students' own writing come to mind: "Oh, I bet Carter could use this format to write something about Minecraft." Mentor texts also teach students *how* to write—from showing them how to structure a piece of writing to demonstrating how to use an em dash to add detail—so they should seem chock-full of possibility.

Mentor Texts Take Many Forms

A mentor text can be *any* text by a professional that inspires and guides student writing, from a single sentence to a whole article or an entire book. A mentor text can be a designed text that combines words and images (like the one you just studied) or a podcast episode or video.

"Good writing makes writers want to write."

—Penny Kittle, *Write Beside Them* (2008, 74)

Mentor Texts Are Accessible

While the writing in a mentor text should be beautiful and inspiring, your students need to be able to read and understand it if they are to see the writer's craft at work. And sometimes the writing isn't too difficult, but the piece is just too long, and you know your students will struggle to make it to the end. If you've fallen for a text that is just a bit too challenging for your readers or just too long, consider excerpting it and giving them a smaller chunk to better support students' comprehension and stamina.

"Tomorrow Is Too Far," from *The Thing Around Your Neck*

by Chimamanda Ngoze Adichie (New York, Anchor, 2010, 187–97)

. . . with writing in it like this . . .

It was the summer you spent in Nigeria, the summer before your parents' divorce, before your mother swore you would never again set foot in Nigeria to see your father's family, especially Grandmama. You remember the heat of that summer clearly, even now, eighteen years later—the way Grandmama's yard felt moistly warm, a yard with so many trees that the telephone wire was tangled in leaves and different branches touched one another and sometimes mangoes appeared on cashew trees and guavas on mango trees. The thick mat of decaying leaves was soggy under your bare feet. In the afternoons, yellow-bellied bees buzzed around your head and your brother Nonso's and cousin Dozie's heads, and in the evening Grandmama let only your brother Nonso climb the trees to shake a loaded branch, although you were a better climber than he was. Fruit would rain down, avocados and cashews and guavas, and you and your cousin Dozie would fill old buckets with them.

It was the summer Grandmama taught Nonso how to pluck the coconuts. The coconut trees were hard to climb, so limb-free and tall, and Grandmama gave Nonso a long stick and showed him how to nudge the padded pods down. . . .

It was the summer you asked Grandmama why Nonso sipped first even though Dozie was thirteen, a year older than Nonso, and Grandmama said Nonso was her son's only son, the one who would carry on the Nnabuisi name, while Dozie was only a *nwadiana*, her daughter's son. (188–89)

*. . . twelfth grader McCall P. wrote a short story,
with writing in it like this:*

Chooses a second-person stance.

Writes about family relationships.

Italicizes words that demonstrate a character's voice.

Uses structural repetition.

That was the summer *you* enthusiastically agreed to travel to South Carolina for a week to watch your five cousins; coincidentally, that was the week the foster baby, Morgan, learned how to climb out of her crib. And the rest of the children learned how to turn off the movie quickly and fake sleep until after you returned Morgan's flailing and screaming body to the crib. That was the week Madison decided she wouldn't eat meat, or anything else that you cooked for dinner, and Manning swore he was allergic to carrots since they left a bad taste in his mouth. That was the week Barnett thought it would be *just kinda silly* if he pushed Johnny off the backyard zipline and Barnett swore *Johnny started it* when he threw fresh eggs from the chicken coop at him.

That was the summer Robert visited you from Connecticut and swore he would never come back. It was the summer you gave him and Emelia permission to play football with the neighbors and

continued on next page

he returned home with swollen ears, puffy eyes, and hives that he itched until his raw skin peeked out from beneath the bumps. It was then that Aunt Beth and Mom rushed him to the hospital, waited there for hours, and eventually found out he had experienced an allergic reaction to yellow jackets.

Long sentences throughout capture the feeling of remembering.

Mentor Texts Help Writing Teachers . . .

Diversify the Teaching Voices in the Classroom

With mentor texts at the center of our writing instruction, we don't have to be everything to every student writer. The writers behind the mentor texts—representing diverse backgrounds and perspectives—are also teachers. Students are more likely to take their writing to the next level when they can learn from writers who look like them, have similar life experiences, and articulate viewpoints like their own.

Teach Writing Authentically

When we gather professional examples of the kind of writing we want our students to create and we study it for structure and craft, the skills that are important to teach come clearly

> " I show up [as a writer] to say, "I am you. You are me. I've been where you are. And hopefully, you're going to succeed far beyond me."
>
> —Jason Reynolds,
> *The Daily Show with Trevor Noah* (2018)

into focus. If the mentor writers layer evidence through hyperlinks, we need to teach our writers to layer evidence through hyperlinks. If the mentor writers conclude by zooming out to the global importance of the issue, we need to teach our writers to do the same. Our instruction is rooted not in curriculum guides and pacing charts, but in the expectations of real-world writing and the needs of our students.

Multiply Instructional Power

With a little experience, students learn that they can find the answers to their writing problems in mentor texts. They learn to turn to these other "teachers" for guidance and often find solutions to their writing problems without even needing our support. With mentor texts, every desk has multiple teachers by its side.

Strengthen the Reading Curriculum

When students study a mentor text to discover ideas, and then return to it to help them organize their thoughts, and then search it again for guidance on crafting stronger sentences, and examine it as they polish their writing, they are digging deep and reading with an engagement that is uncommon in most reading curricula.

Streamline Planning and Reduce Instructional Decision Fatigue

Instead of spending hours reinventing the wheel with each unit (or spending money to buy units from others), we can rely on the planning routine we use with mentor texts to work for every kind of writing we need to teach—both genres we know by heart and genres we've never taught before. It works for first-grade writers and college writers. It's the safe, simple place we return to each time we need to plan a writing unit.

If you ask one simple question of everything you read—"What could this piece help my students do in their writing?"—you will find mentor texts literally *everywhere*:

- in the literature you already teach
- in your own pleasure reading
- in the articles you stumble across online
- in go-to spots that consistently yield great mentor texts
- in conversations and exchanges with other teachers who also use mentor texts.

After studying this opinion piece . . .

New York Has a Great Subway, if You're Not in a Wheelchair

by Sasha Blair-Goldensohn, *The New York Times* (March 29, 2017)

. . . with writing in it like this . . .

Nearly eight years ago, on a bright summer morning in Manhattan, I was walking through Central Park when an enormous rotted tree branch snapped and fell on my head.

What came next was a remarkable turn of events that saved my life. First, a doctor out for a morning jog saw me lying unconscious, and used a pair of jeans he dug out of my backpack to slow the bleeding until an ambulance came.

This is my life . . .

Bedroom

5:45 AM

It is dark outside.

Features a short, arresting beginning with longer paragraphs to follow.

The frigid floor bites the soles of my feet as I struggle to get out of bed. I have hit the snooze twice, but my body aches with exhaustion. I have been asleep for only six hours because of the ridiculous history essay I had to write. Who cares about that stupid queen that had a giant palace during the French Revolution? My life would be filled with eternal sunshine and rainbows if I could just sleep for another hour. School needs to start later.

Starts with a microstory as a way into opinion writing.

Here are the facts, not the myths that have been created about teenagers and sleeping habits. You have all heard these lies a multitude of times, such as, that teenagers are lazy and irresponsible for not going to bed early? These are lies, so the next time someone tells you that you are lazy or careless because of your sleeping patterns, you can look them in the face and prove them wrong with cold, hard facts.

Introduces idea of dispelling common myths.

Mentor Texts Help Student Writers . . .

Practice Authentic Patterns of Learning

Studying mentor texts isn't a school skill; it's a life skill. If we want to learn to do anything better, we study the work of experts—whether it's Ina Garten baking a tart on TV or Steph Curry making a three-pointer. We watch those we admire in action, take note, and then try it ourselves. Learning to write is a similarly intuited "craft apprenticeship" (Ray 1999, 10).

Build Writing Identity

When we study mentor texts with our students, we invite them to pull up a seat at the same table as the pros, and we send the message, "Yep, you can do that, too, because you're a writer." When students see themselves this way, they are able to play, take risks, and add their voice to a larger community of working writers.

Make Authentic Writing

Professional writers in the wild compose poems and op-eds and short stories and reviews and essays and listicles and feature articles. They don't write "five-paragraph essays" or "research papers"—school writing. We can prepare our students for academic writing tasks when we invite them to make the kind of writing real writers make.

> "Students who see how other writers shoot their free throws will be more likely to succeed when it becomes time for them to shoot their own."
>
> —Kelly Gallagher,
> *Teaching Adolescent Writers* (2006, 76)

Face Future Writing Challenges

We can't prepare students for every kind of academic, personal, and professional writing they will need to do in their lives. But we can teach them the transferable skill of reading like writers and finding the craft and structure they need for the writing task at hand. With ample practice, students will know how to find and use mentor texts whenever they *need* them—to write a paper for a professor or a memo for a boss, for example.

SPOTLIGHT ON
STUDENT WORK

After studying these graphic novels . . .

Drowned City: Hurricane Katrina and New Orleans

by Don Brown (Boston, MA: HMH Books, 2017)

The Unwanted: Stories of the Syrian Refugees

by Don Brown (Boston, MA: HMH Books, 2018)

. . . with writing and illustrating in it like this . . .

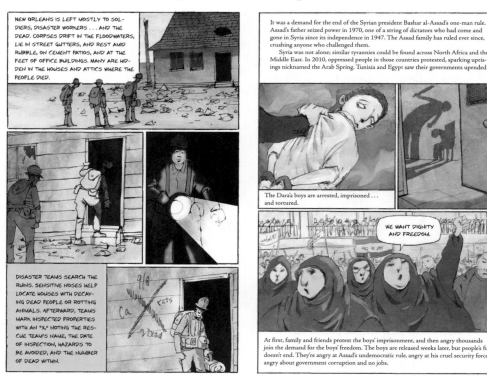

Structure: one box at the top, a few boxes across in the middle, and one large box at the bottom.

Features physical positioning of characters in relation to one another to show perspective.

Zooms in on characters' reactions to show tension.

Relies on illustration rather than dialogue to tell the story.

chapter two

TEACHING

Students

A powerful
simile

TO READ LIKE

Writers

All writing is a reflection of decision making. Writers choose every word and punctuation mark, and they also decide the best order for their words and ideas. When we read like writers, we notice the decisions writers have made, like the ones in this poem by Clint Smith. Take a few moments to read it, then grab a pen and mark it up! Jot some notes in the margin about what you notice about the decisions Smith made.

VIDEO 2–1

Here's what we noticed when we read Clint Smith's poem like writers.

Something You Should Know

is that as a kid, I once worked at a pet store.
I cleaned the cages
of small animals like turtles, hamsters,
rabbits, and hermit crabs.
I watched the hermit crab continue
to grow, molt, shed its skin and scurry across
the bottom of the aquarium to find a new shell.
Which left me afraid for the small creature,
to run around all exposed that way, to have
to live its entire life requiring something else
to feel safe. Perhaps that is when I became afraid
of needing anything beyond myself. Perhaps
that is why, even now, I can want so desperately
to show you all of my skin, but am more afraid
of meeting you, exposed, in open water.

Clint Smith
(*Counting Descent*, 2016)

Did you notice some of the same moves we did? Writers are apt to notice how something is written any time they read, whether it's a Clint Smith poem or the copy in an L. L. Bean catalog. They can't help but notice, because their own writing and decision making are never far from their thinking, even when they read. *Especially* when they read.

Most of our students, however, do not come to us reading like writers. They don't know how to notice something about the craft or structure of a text, so we have to show them what happens in writers' minds when they read.

First, Read Like Readers

Their whole academic lives, our students have been reading as readers. They know how to ask questions, offer predictions, make connections, and share emotional and intellectual responses to texts. This is how most people read, of course. They read for meaning. We want our students to continue to enjoy reading as they always have, so welcoming their readerly responses to texts comes first.

> You know, I read stuff over and over. And it made deep sense. I think what happened was the language settled in me. . . . From a really young age, I was reading like a writer. I was reading for this deep understanding of the literature not simply to hear the story but to understand how the author got the story on the page.
>
> —Jacqueline Woodson, *Fresh Air* (2014)

Next, Introduce Students to a Different Way of Reading

Explain that writers read differently than people who aren't writers, just like interior designers study rooms differently than people who aren't designers, and makeup artists study people's faces differently than people who aren't makeup artists. Makers of all kinds see the world through their particular lens, and reading like a writer isn't just something we do in English class. It's a real-world skill.

VIDEO 2–2
Introducing Students to a Different Way of Reading

Then, Share the Process

When experienced writers read and something strikes them, they are noticing, theorizing, naming, and writing in their minds all at once. The process looks something like this:

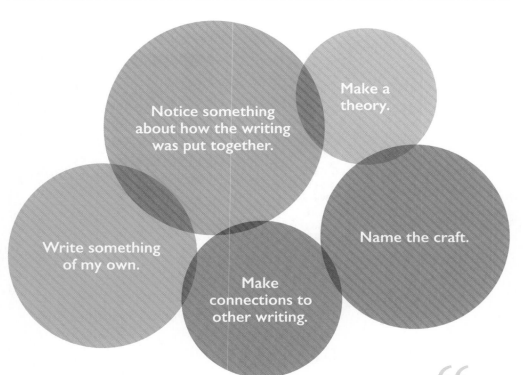

Reading like a Writer as a Habit of Mind

- Notice something about how the writing was put together.
- Make a theory.
- Write something of my own.
- Make connections to other writing.
- Name the craft.

Consider asking students to bring in examples of how they read the world through a particular lens. For instance, students who play an instrument might play a video clip of a favorite musician and explain what they notice about their technique. Student athletes might play short excerpts from professional games and talk through the players' moves. Then have them share how learning from these experts impacts their own work. Invite your students' passions into the classroom and let them show you how they read the world differently.

> " [Students] must read like a writer in order to learn how to write like a writer. There is no other way in which the intricate complexity of a writer's knowledge can be acquired. "
>
> —Frank Smith, *Joining the Literacy Club* (1987, 23)

But for teaching purposes, it's helpful to envision the process of reading like a writer more like four steps on a staircase. We want to get to the top, where our students are making intentional decisions about their own writing. To get there, we move through a series of clearly defined steps.

The Steps of Reading Like a Writer

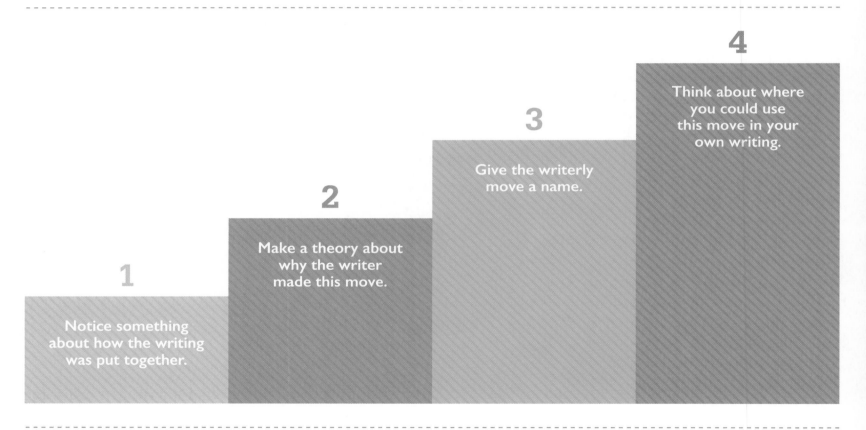

1 Notice something about how the writing was put together.

2 Make a theory about why the writer made this move.

3 Give the writerly move a name.

4 Think about where you could use this move in your own writing.

(adapted from Katie Wood Ray, *Wondrous Words*, 1999, 120)

Step One: Notice Something About How a Text Is Written

Let's say you're studying the Clint Smith poem with your students. You've responded to it as readers, and now students have it in hand or can see it projected on a whiteboard. You might begin by sharing something you notice, such as how the title spills over into the first line of the poem. Then, invite your students to notice along with you, and record their noticings on the board, a giant sticky note, or around the poem on a document camera.

Now, be prepared. When you first ask students what they notice about a text, they might not see much of anything, but you can guide them with two simple practices:

- Encourage students to point with their finger to a place in the text where they notice a writing move. This keeps them from responding with generalities ("It just flows"), and it encourages them to notice things they don't know the technical name for.
- Encourage students to start by noticing the small, obvious things—for example, the exclamation point at the end of the sentence or the paragraph that begins with *and*. No noticing is too small because every word and every punctuation mark was intentionally chosen by the writer.

VIDEO 2–3
Noticing How a Text Is Written

Q: *I am struggling to get students to see more complex author moves in texts. Even after I model identifying more complex choices, they still revert back to labeling sections of text with "good description" and "interesting word choice." How do I get them to see more?*

A: We see this all the time! To help students name craft moves with more specificity, we encourage them to reframe their noticings as *directions to themselves*. For example, a student may share that the Clint Smith poem has "a powerful ending," and while this is true, it doesn't tell the writer how to bring this craft move into their own writing. But, if we reframe this idea as directions, we know a writer can end by

- slowing down and stretching the writing out with lots of commas,
- using the introspective word *perhaps* to share an important theme, or
- returning to an image from the beginning of the poem.

Step Two: Make a Theory

As students begin to notice how a text is written, the next step is to think about the writer's decisions. Why does Smith use second person in this poem? Why does he repeat the word *afraid*? Why does he break the line after *desperately*? We can't know the answers to these questions for certain, of course, but finding the "right" answer isn't the point. The point is to get curious about a writer's decisions so we learn to make more intentional choices in our own work.

In this step, if we can, it helps to think of other texts where we have seen these same writerly moves. For example, these four poems we found on Billy Collins' Poetry 180 website have titles that spill over into the first line of the poem and leave you wanting to know more, just like Smith's title:

> "Girls, Look Out for Todd Bernstein," by Jason Bredle
>
> "Did I Miss Anything?" by Tom Wayman
>
> "Neglect," by R. T. Smith
>
> "A Man I Knew," by Margaret Levine

When students see the same craft move used by different writers, it helps them understand that a writer's craft choices are individual but not unique (Ray 1999). Different writers use language in the exact same ways for effect—and so can they!

Now, when you are new to teaching with mentor texts, you might have trouble thinking of other examples where writers are making the same moves. That's okay. The more you read with your students, the more connections you will make across texts. But at first, if you want to show your students different writers using the same techniques, search for examples before the lesson so you have them at the ready.

> "In order to gather a repertoire of craft possibilities that will help a writer write well, that writer first has to learn how to read differently, how to read with a sense of possibility, a sense of "What do I see here that might work for me in my writing?" This is what reading like a writer means— to read with a sense of possibility."
>
> —Katie Wood Ray, *Wondrous Words* (1999, 12)

VIDEO 2–4
Making a Theory

Step Three: Name the Craft

When we are theorizing about a move a writer has made, we use words that make sense to us and that clarify its purpose. Eventually, we settle on a name for the move so we have common language for talking about texts. To do this, we listen carefully. For example, if students are discussing the title of Smith's poem and one of them says, "It's like he wants us to have to read the second line to figure it out. He leaves us hanging," we can take this language and repackage it as the name for a writerly move: it's a *leave-me-hanging title*.

Sometimes students will notice a craft move that has an actual name. For example, if students are noticing the many *s* sounds that Smith uses throughout the poem, we can—in the most authentic way—teach them the terms *alliteration* and *consonance*. There is value in knowing classic terminology. However, what's more important is that students can identify writers' choices and name them in a way that clarifies their purpose. After all, writers don't draft and revise with terms in mind, but with intentions.

Step Four: Think About Using This Move in Your Own Writing

When students are first learning to read like writers, we invite them to try something they've noticed right away—either in their notebook or with an existing draft. This concrete, in-the-moment application helps students connect the dots of the process, and they don't have to do anything else with these little writing exercises except make and share them.

VIDEO 2–5
Naming Craft

VIDEO 2–6
Using a Move in Your Own Writing

Rebekah gave students some time to write under the influence of "Something You Should Know." Notice the variety of moves they tried.

Craft Move: Thoughtful line breaks

Something you should know

is that when I was a kid, I would help my mom prune flowers

I snipped the dead ones

but observed the buds that were shut up tight

—June H.

Something that you should know is that when I was
younger, I remember watching a movie about birds.
My favorite part was the scene about the owls. The
silent but powerful creatures that only come out for
a short amount of time.

—Mathias R.

Craft Move: Intentional fragment

Something You Should Know

is that as a kid, I once loved space.

I examined the facts

of the planets like Jupiter, Mercury, Mars, and Pluto.

—Juliet F.

Craft Move:
Items in a list with
classic punctuation

Something you should know is that I dislike rainy days.

I hate to walk through them with all of the puddles, the

feeling of water in my sock, and the way my hair gets soggy.

—Jonah M.

Craft Move:
Magic-three
sentence

Perhaps that is why I take losing badly, and my parents would know. Perhaps that is why, even now, I don't want to stop competing—even when the game's over, the last shot had been taken, the final pass had been made.

—*Ryan L.*

Perhaps that is why I master the unmastered. Perhaps that is why, even now, I can want so desperately to unlock my last achievement, complete my final goal, finish what I started.

—*Foster S.*

In our experience, most students will not begin crafting their own writing with intention unless they are explicitly invited to, and at first, their attempts can seem awkward and ungraceful. They need the mentor text right next to them, and they sometimes copy the move word by word or sentence by sentence. But with practice, they don't have to think about it so much and the process of reading like a writer becomes more natural.

Reading like a writer can feel a bit abstract. In this resource you'll find five supports to make the process more tangible and concrete. Offer them to individual students, small groups, or the whole class to help build confidence and provide practice in a more hands-on, makerspace-inspired way.

ONLINE RESOURCE 2–1

Five Supports for Reading Like Writers

Reading like a writer can feel a bit abstract. Here are some ways to make the process more tangible and concrete. Offer these supports to individual students, small groups, or the whole class to help them build confidence and gain practice in a more hands-on, makerspace-inspired way.

Build It

How-To

1. Gather loose parts such as Legos, small blocks, and wooden beads. Provide enough for small groups of students to have plenty of materials to build one or more creations. Consider placing the loose parts in small divided trays for easy handling and cleanup.

2. Project a mentor sentence for the class to study. Invite students to jot what they notice in their notebooks.

3. After sharing out, introduce the students to the loose parts, and invite them to build a representation of the sentence using what they have noticed.

4. To close, ask students to give their build a name that describes the kind of sentence they have studied. They can use this sentence frame to present their build: *This is a _____ sentence because _____.*

An Example

In an eighth-grade English class, students studied this claim from a mentor text:

Hence my main point: The Night King is dull as dishwater.

—David Sims, Spencer Kornhaber, and Lenika Cruz, "The Long Night Finally Arrives on *Game of Thrones*" (*The Atlantic*, April 29, 2019, www.theatlantic.com/entertainment/archive/2019/04/game-thrones-season-8-episode-3-the-long-night-review/588247/)

As a class, students noticed the following:

- There is a colon that points from the lead-up to the big idea of the sentence.
- The writer uses a simile in the claim.
- *Dull* and *dishwater* are alliterative.
- The word *hence* indicates that a lot of information came before this claim, and now the writer is using the claim to summarize his main point in succinct terms.

Then, students built and named their builds (see Figures 2–1a and 2–1b.)

Variations

Students can also make builds that represent

- a paragraph,
- a whole piece of writing, or
- a genre of writing.

Graph It

How-To

This is a catapult claim because the first part of the sentence catapults the claim over the colon.

This is a drumroll suspense claim because the first part of the sentence (the yellow bricks) act like a drumroll leading up to the colon (the white door). That creates suspense, but when you open the door, you see the claim.

For More Information

Our friend Angela Stockman has written extensively and fascinatingly(!) about using loose parts in writing classroom.

- Check out the post "Confronting Print Barriers in the Writing Workshop and Leveraging Loose Parts" on her blog, www.angelastockman.com (March 22, 2019).
- And find even more ideas in her books: *Hacking the Writing Workshop: Redesign with Making in Mind* (South Euclid: Times, 2018) and *Make Writing: 5 Teaching Strategies That Turn Writer's Workshop into a Maker's Space* (South Euclid: Times 10, 2015).

chapter three

Learning ABOUT Craft AND Punctuation

suggests that punctuation is related to craft

Wh…hen we study craft and punctuation, we study the artful ways writers choose and mix words, build sentences, and add punctuation to guide the way readers experience a text. When introducing our students to mentor texts, we start with craft rather than whole pieces of writing because craft crosses all genres, topics, and audiences of writing. It also helps to start small. A beautifully crafted sentence is filled with interesting decisions the writer has made, and there's so much to learn. Consider this sentence, for example, from the opening pages of Sarah Pennypacker's beautiful novel *Pax* (New York: Balzer and Bray, 2016). Grab your pen again and make notes about what you notice.

The sharp odor of pine—wood, bark, cones, and needles—slivered through the air like blades, but beneath that, the fox recognized softer clover and wild garlic and ferns, and also a hundred things he had never encountered before but that smelled green and urgent.

(Balzer and Bray, 2016 1–2)

VIDEO 3–1

See what we noticed when we read Pennypacker's sentence like writers.

Spring training invites romance.
It's the basis of the seasonal vocabulary, all
rebirth and growth and optimism. But this
invitation is incidental: Spring training, if
it is going to be at all enjoyable, *requires*
romance.

(*Sports Illustrated*, February 27, 2020)

When we studied this sentence with our students, they noticed the repetition of conjunctions in close succession, "softer clover and wild garlic and ferns," a craft move known as polysyndeton. A polysyndeton conjoins important words and ideas. It also affects the pace of writing, forcing the reader to linger just a bit longer than usual. In Pennypacker's sentence, the polysyndeton mimics the ambling path of the fox.

This craft move works beautifully in a young adult novel, but we also see it in all kinds of genres in the wild. For example, take a look at this polysyndeton from Emma Baccellieri's piece "Embracing the Romance of Spring Training." See excerpt on the left.

A craft study of a sentence like Pennypacker's can help students write stronger sentences in *any* piece of writing. Consider how her lists of concrete nouns might help students bring more specificity to their ideas or how her use of em dashes might help them vary sentence structure in a piece of analytical writing.

> "Every so often I'll hear writers say that there are other writers they would read if for no other reason than to marvel at the skill with which they can put together the sort of sentences that move us to read closely, to disassemble and reassemble them, much the way a mechanic might learn about an engine by taking it apart. The well-made sentence transcends time and genre."
>
> —Francine Prose, *Reading Like a Writer* (2007, 36)

How to Study a Mentor Text at the Word, Line, or Sentence Level

We like to reserve about ten minutes at the beginning of each class period for craft study because it sets the tone for the work ahead. But craft studies—both planned and impromptu—can happen anytime we're reading together. And if you don't have ten minutes a day? No worries. Just fit it in as often as you can. Even one solid craft study a week would greatly benefit your writers.

The table here shows what we do in the ten minutes of study after we've selected a sentence (or a few sentences if they are working together).

A Process for Craft and Punctuation Study

1	2	3	4	5
Introduce the Mentor Sentence	**Notice**	**Share**	**Try It**	**Share Again**
Project the sentence onto the whiteboard and have students copy it into their notebooks, skipping lines. For longer sentences, consider making a typed-up handout, which students can glue in a notebook, double or triple spaced so they have room to make notes. Share some information about the author and the text, then read the sentence aloud.	Ask students what they notice about the craft of the sentence and why the writer might have made these choices. Give them a few minutes to jot down their observations.	Invite students to share what they noticed, and record the list on the board, on a giant sticky note, or on an online notepad like blankslate.io. If there's something you want to teach that students didn't notice, go ahead and point it out.	Invite students to open their notebooks and write a sentence that is like the one they have just studied. They can also practice by rewriting a sentence in an existing draft, if it makes sense.	Invite students to share their sentences and listen to how their classmates translated the craft of the mentor text into their own writing.

Q: *So if craft crosses all genres, topics, and audiences, do I need to match my mentor texts to what students are writing about—their topics?*

A: No, you don't. Hopefully your students are choosing their own topics, so even if you tried to find same-topic mentor texts for each student, you'd need hundreds of them for every unit. This isn't reasonable; you can't do it. Also, you want students to borrow writers' craft, not their thinking, so your text selection should show students that craft is generalizable and that excellent writing on any topic can guide their writing on the topic they have chosen.

Guiding Questions for Studying Craft and Punctuation

If the question "What do you notice?" seems too big and open-ended, here are some variations of this question you can offer:

What parts of this sentence do you admire?

What words stand out to you? Why?

Can you spot any interesting punctuation? How would the sentence change if the punctuation were different?

Does this line or sentence remind you of other writing?

Does this sentence contain a helpful pattern or template for your own work?

How might you use this sentence to inspire one of your own?

Seventh-grade students practice incorporating
Pennypacker's craft moves into their own sentences.

The soft smell of a football—leather, laces, and familiarity—shivered through the air.

—Roman G.

The hard odor of shotgun shells, gunpowder and dead birds lingers in the air, along with the smell of wet green grass on a cool spring morning.

—Jack N.

The sharp odor of rain —metallic, raw, and wet— filled the air like water, but under that, something else from the sky that was musty and dry.

—Matthew W.

The sweet smell of flowers hit me—the pollen, the sweet nectar, the petals— came at me like a cloud of perfume, but beneath that smell the softer smell of mulch and grass and leaves.

—Sarah Carter N.

The fragrance of the cupcakes—lemon zest, milk, powdered sugar, and chocolate—wafted through the kitchen, but hidden by that, I recognized something deeper, burnt sugar stuck to the oven, and a mesmerizing heat that caused sweat to form on my brow.

—Magovern R.

The strong odor of the forest—decaying leaves, blooming flowers, and mushrooms—inscribed itself into the air like hieroglyphics in a pyramid.

—Gretchen G.

Quick Ways to Share Sentences

- Read your sentence to a partner or small group.
- Stand in a circle while each person reads their sentence slowly and clearly without commentary in between.
- Share your sentence on a Padlet wall (https://padlet.com).
- Write your sentence on a sticky note, find a wall to stick it on, and walk around the classroom, reading others' sentences. Put stars or stickers on your favorites.
- Write your sentence on an index card, and put it facedown in a pile in the middle of the classroom. When everyone has added their sentence to the pile, draw a random card and read the sentence out loud. Students can have fun guessing the author of each sentence or can celebrate anonymously!
- Bring your notebook up to the document camera, share your writing, and talk about your process of moving from studying the mentor to getting words on a page.

When we are first introducing how to read like a writer at the beginning of the year, we spend more time in craft study, and one way to slow the process down is to do just one step each day.

Craft Study Across the Week

M	Invitation to Notice	Project a sentence and have students jot down their noticings.
T	Invitation to Discuss	Have students share their noticings and discuss why they think the author made these choices.
W	Invitation to Research	Have students look in their independent reading books or previously studied mentor texts for additional examples of the craft moves in the mentor sentence.
TH	Invitation to Write	Invite students to write their own sentences or revise existing sentences.
F	Invitation to Share	Allow students to revise their sentences and share them in a variety of ways.

ONLINE RESOURCE 3–1
Look here for a blank chart students can use to record their findings in a weeklong craft study.

> **One of the clearest ways to define brush strokes for students is by showing models and having them imitate.**
>
> —Harry Noden, *Image Grammar* (2011, 5)

The
Writer's Notebook

There are a few tools we can't live without in our writing classrooms, and writers' notebooks—those dog-eared, coffee-stained, ink-smeared journals that never leave a writer's side—are one of them. Our students start writing in notebooks during the first week of school, and the journals quickly become beloved storehouses for all things writing: ideas, doodles, seeds for future writing, questions, writing lessons, crafting techniques, mentor texts.

Students design and organize their notebooks (paper or digital) in a way that best supports them as writers, and they do all of their daily craft study exploration and practice in a designated section of the notebook.

What is the author doing?	Why is the author doing this?	What can I call this crafting technique?	Have I ever seen another author craft this way?	Examples of this technique in my writing?
Word Choice: Shower "The result was good, but not quite good enough, so in went a flurry of grated Parmesan for savory depth, and a shower of lemon juice, to lend some tart, shimmery brightness." Helen Rosner "The Many Lives of Roberto: A Soup" <u>New Yorker</u>	To deepen the "snow" diction: flurry and shower For the timid cook, "shower" suggests a very healthy squeeze of lemon or perhaps lemons	Unexpected Verbs or Borrowed Verbs (She's using "snowy" words to describe food prep)	"While I had been napping out in that park, while I'd been playing back memories of him in the low-lit corners of my mind, he had been excavating me, digging to the center of my soul." Emily X.R. Pan <u>The Astonishing Color of After</u> p. 152 The surprising verb "excavating" followed by another construction word, "digging"	I want to use a dance word arabesque—to describe the movements of the birds above my house in my memoir.

A Chart for Recording Craft Study in the Notebook

ONLINE RESOURCE 3–2

Here you'll find Gallery of Craft and Punctuation Moves examples (plus more!) organized and ready for you to copy or project and use in your classroom.

ONLINE RESOURCE 3–3

You'll find a blank craft study chart your students can use here.

Gallery OF Craft AND Punctuation Moves

VIDEO 3–2
How to Use the Galleries

In the gallery that follows, we share some of the craft moves we see again and again as we study excellent writing. This gallery will help you get started teaching with mentor texts right away and finding great texts of your own. The gallery is divided into five categories, though many moves create overlapping effects—a specific word choice affects voice, for instance, or a punctuation decision impacts the design of a sentence. But categorizing them is still helpful as we work to understand the new examples we encounter along the way.

Writers are word artists. Like a painter with his palette, a writer plays around with different words to see their effect on a sentence. A single word can bring a whole sentence to life . . . or it can just as easily diminish it.

This Word, Not That

Writers often choose one word over another because of its connotation, or the feelings and images the word conjures. Two words may have the same dictionary definition (denotation) but have different connotations. Writers also choose words for their *music*, or what they sound like when read aloud.

Herbs, plucked off their stems and gently sliced. The more traditional instruction is *concasser*—whacking your herbs into a near-pulp—but I prefer the texture that comes from *ciseler*, the method of rolling, say, parsley leaves into a sloppy imitation of a tube, then slicing across to form mini green chisels.

—Bill Buford, "Mastering the Art of Making a French Omelette," *The New Yorker* (April 18, 2020)

Whack—what an unexpected word choice for a food essay in the *New Yorker*! Why not *crush* or *pluck* (the words given in translation)? *Whack* shares sounds with *pluck*, used earlier in the passage, and presents a stark contrast to the softer image that follows it of rolling and slicing the herb to form tiny shreds.

DIY Words

Sometimes writers invent new words (hello, Shakespeare!) when they can't find a single word to explain what they mean.

Happysad combines two opposites in a surprising way.

I was a liar; a cheater; a manipulator; a fat, happysad, bald-headed black boy with a heart murmur; and according to you and the white girl I lied to every day, I was a good dude.

—Kiese Laymon, *Heavy: An American Memoir* (New York: Scribner, 2018, 103)

Check out these two magical books dedicated to tracking fledgling words:

- *The Emotionary: A Dictionary of Words That Don't Exist for Feelings That Do,* by Eden Sher
- *The Dictionary of Obscure Sorrows* (www.dictionaryofobscuresorrows.com)

Hyphenated Words

Sometimes writers string together a few words or hyphenate the words of a phrase to communicate an idea more powerfully.

Here the new word is a noun . . .

She's been running for who knows how long, and it starts to get dark. It's metaphor-darkness, but it's also just the truth.

—Deb Caletti, *A Heart in a Body in the World* (New York, Simon Pulse: 2018, 2)

Now, there's voice-of-a-generation energy around her.

—Craig Jenkins, "The Tide Has Rapidly Turned on Billie Eilish," *Vulture* (February 6, 2020)

. . . and here it's an adjective.

Lingo

Writers use lingo—the vocabulary of a particular subject—to add authority to their writing. Lingo consists of the words and kinds of words that show up again and again, words such as *woozy*, as used to describe music.

How would you define woozy after reading these three examples?

The woozy, lyrically dense songs have the feel of "ciphers"—hip-hop's tradition in which small groups of rappers improvise and feed off one another in a live setting.

—Carrie Battan, "Ed Sheeran and Friends," *The New Yorker* (July 22, 2019)

Over a bed of woozy synths and strings, Grande sings delicately about a situation she described succinctly to a fan on Twitter as, "feeling badly for the person you're with because you love somebody else."

—Craig Jenkins, "*Thank U, Next* Is a Phoenix Moment for Ariana Grande," *Vulture* (February 8, 2019)

Her rise has been striking: At 14, she put the song "Ocean Eyes" on SoundCloud, a glassy, straightforward ballad with tearful synths and woozy, Lana Del Rey-indebted crooning.

—Stacey Anderson, *When We All Fall Asleep, Where Do We Go?* review, *Pitchfork* (March 29, 2019)

On Twitter, use #mentortext #writingwithmentors to find an abundance of mentor texts that are updated frequently. Or go to our website, www.movingwriters.org, where you can access a "mentor text dropbox" organized by craft and genre and vetted by fellow classroom teachers.

Interesting Images

Writers use images to connect with their readers, and it's often the unexpected combination of sensory details, or the never-been-written-before metaphor, that makes us think while reading, "I know exactly what that's like."

Synesthesia

Synesthesia is the mixing of senses. It's an actual human condition—for example, some people can smell color—but it's also a strategy that writers can employ to get at the hard-to-describe quality of a thing.

> Where I was that day: on the old tweed couch in Axel's basement, brushing against his shoulder, trying to ignore the orange wall of electricity between us.
>
> —Emily X.R. Pan, *The Astonishing Color of After* (New York, Little, Brown and Company: 2018, 17)

Here the synesthesia is in a noun phrase . . .

> I was jealous of how he watched Hazel, drinking in her music like water and tasting how she dissolved herself in it like a sugar cube.
>
> —Julie Berry, *Lovely War* (New York: Penguin Books, 2019, 19)

. . . and here it's captured by verbs.

Sentences That Taste and Smell

Writers often rely on the sense of sight to engage the reader, but sometimes they draw on other senses—smell or taste, for instance—to bring a sentence to life.

Notice how the writer seesaws between visual, tactile, and auditory images to create a vibrant, multidimensional snapshot of nature.

Yes, the extinction tables show a mounting tally, and yet there is still the hoot of owls in the evening, still the flash of orange as monarch butterflies make their way north with the spring, still the boil of water before a fluke breaks the surface.

—Bill McKibben, "Fifty Years Past the First Earth Day, a Frayed Planet—and a Sublime One," *The New Yorker* (April 22, 2020)

Comparisons

Writers use comparisons to help readers better understand something or see it in a new way.

At the end of the day, the jar is sucked upward to a vault through a transparent pneumatic tube—a process that evokes the Augustus Gloop scene from "Charlie and the Chocolate Factory."

—Ed Caesar, "The Rock," *The New Yorker* (February 3, 2020, 32)

Sometimes the comparison is a cultural reference.

Meaningful Repetition

One of the most essential tools in the writer's toolbox, repetition helps emphasize ideas, clarify meaning, and create rhythm.

Repetition of a Word or Phrase

Sometimes writers simply repeat words and phrases for emphasis.

With these long legs I'm taken for twelve or thirteen, even a little older. No one ever guesses eleven going on twelve on their first try. More than my long legs, I'm sure it's my plain face that throws them off. Not plain as in homely plain, but *even* plain. Steady. I'm not nine or seven and given to squealing or oohing like Vonetta and Fern. I just let my plain face and plain words speak for me. That way, no one ever says, "Huh?" to me. They know exactly what I mean.

—Rita Williams-Garcia, *One Crazy Summer*
(New York: Amistad, 2010, 8)

The author uses the word plain six times in this short paragraph. Six! Surely that's a decision worth noticing and talking about.

Some teachers ask their students to glue all of their mentor texts, including multipage articles, into their writers' notebooks for safekeeping. Longer articles can be reduced from letter size to fit snugly in between the pages of a more streamlined notebook.

Say-It-Again Sentences

Sometimes writers unpack or clarify their ideas by saying the same thing twice but in slightly different words—a technique known as *expolitio*.

This excerpt is structured like a little argument: main point, supporting examples, then reiteration of the main point—twice!

Rose Lavelle is made for metaphor.

Depending on the day, Lavelle may be an escape artist, wriggling out of tight spots; a virtuoso, known for her creativity; or a trickster, skilled in deceit. She may be a magician, or a technically flawless cyborg, or a purveyor of fine spices focused on nutmeg. At her best, she may be all of these at once. But to be familiar with her work is to understand that the figurative language is necessary. To watch Lavelle play is to feel the limits of any literal vocabulary. She demands new terms.

—Emma Baccellieri, "How Rose Lavelle Found Her Joy," *Sports Illustrated* (March 5, 2020)

I miss sports. I miss millionaires diving into billionaires to save a $150 basketball. I miss buzzer beaters, chin-high heaters, and even Astros cheaters. I miss one seeds and three putts and five holes. I miss Roger Federer faking his opponent so far the wrong way on a forehand that both guys have to laugh.

—Rick Reilly, "I Miss Sports So, So, So Much," *The Atlantic* (March 20, 2020)

Anaphora

We tend to think of anaphora, the deliberate repetition of the first part of a sentence, as a poetic device, but nonfiction and fiction writers use it to create rhythm and emphasis just like poets do.

The anaphora is also a structural device.

Powerful sentences come in all shapes and sizes. Some are short, some are long, and some are so long and so complex they make you pause and wonder, "Is this the *same* sentence?"

Magic-Three Sentences

There's something about three that's magical, and writers often cluster words, ideas, or images together in threes.

> To think, only yesterday I was in chancletas, sipping lemonade and watching my twin cousins run through the sprinkler in the yard.
>
> —Meg Medina, *Merci Suárez Changes Gears* (Somerville, Candlewick: 2018, 6)

Three strong visual images. Notice how, rhythmically, the third item in the list is the longest. Think about how different it would sound to move the longer phrase into a different position!

Lists

Lists inside sentences help writers add specific details, create rhythm, and write concisely.

> There's been some small amount of winning, here and there, but just really a *tremendous lot* of dying—characters big and small, both the beloved and the benighted, have been poisoned, beheaded, slashed, gashed, stabbed, devoured by hounds, hurled from parapets, immolated, head-squished, pincushioned by arrows and—in one case—even died of old age, if you can imagine anything so grotesque.
>
> —Glen Weldon, "Which Characters Will Lose the 'Game of Thrones?': A Chronicle of Many Deaths Foretold," *Pop Culture Happy Hour*, NPR (April 10, 2019)

The length and the pace of this list mimic the action of a thrilling battle scene.

Contrasting Lengths

Making writing is a lot like making music, and some writers will play with sentence length to create a kind of rhythm on the page. A really short sentence after a few long sentences can really pop! Several short sentences in a row can create the feeling of jumpiness or being out of breath.

The contrasting short sentence sets up the writer's claim.

It is hard to know where sports fit into society in the time of the coronavirus. That will take time. But it's easier to see how sports fit into the story of the coronavirus.

—Michael Rosenburg, "It Helps Society to Know Which Athletes Are Battling Coronavirus," *Sports Illustrated* (March 19, 2020)

Contrasting Types

Writers mix simple, compound, and complex sentences, along with questions and intentional fragments, to create variety and hold the reader's attention.

The writer punctuates these gorgeous declarative sentences with an even more gorgeous question.

The stars actually twinkled. . . . They danced in place with such energy that I swear I heard them rustling—or was that the breeze in the ten thousand breathing leaves?

—Barbara Brown Taylor, *Leaving Church: A Memoir of Faith* (New York: HarperOne, 2006, 58)

Sentences That Begin with a Conjunction

Used intentionally and sparingly, sentences that begin with a conjunction can help a writer connect ideas, control tone, and vary sentence structure.

On iTunes, I've lined up every version I own of one of the seminal hymns of my church, a song that right now, I simply need to hear. I work to the sound of Lou Rawls and Reba McEntire singing it, Aaron Neville and Al Green singing it, Aretha herself singing it, voice strong, righteous and true. Because, yes, grace is confusing and unsettling. But it is amazing, too.

—Leonard Pitts Jr., "I Survived a Fire in My Home, but It Could Have Been So Much Worse," *Miami Herald* (March 22, 2019)

Sentences that begin with a conjunction aren't always powerful on their own. Their power is in their connection to the ideas that come before them.

Authentic Voice

When students wonder why their writing doesn't sound right, they intuitively know it lacks voice. We must teach into this intuition with mentor texts that model voice-filled writing. Where do you hear the writer speaking directly to you? Where is the person behind the writing?

Talking to Your Reader

Sometimes writers speak directly to their readers. It can catch us off guard and make us pay attention in a different way.

These are imperative sentences with the understood you as the subject.

> Go ahead, click. Treat yourself. Make your day better. Then come back, I'll still be here. . . .
>
> —Glen Weldon, "'The Lion King' Had the Perfect Villain Song. This Time, 'Be Prepared' for Less," *Pop Culture Happy Hour*, NPR (July 17, 2019)

Code-Mixing

Sometimes authors weave together different languages to create a more authentic voice and precise meaning (what is captured in one language isn't always possible in another).

> Everyone who lived and worked on El Rancho de las Rosas was gathered at the edge of the field: Esperanza's family, the house servants in their long white aprons, the vaqueros already sitting on their horses ready to ride out to the cattle, and fifty or sixty campesinos, straw hats in their hands, holding their own knives ready.
>
> —Pam Muñoz Ryan, *Esperanza Rising* (New York, Scholastic: 2002, 4–5)

Notice how the Spanish nouns bring such vividness to the scene.

Showing Vulnerability

Traditionally, students have been taught to leave themselves out of "more formal" genres, but writers in the wild often share their own experiences and feelings as they connect readers to their subject.

When you're a kid, a black- or brown- or yellow- or red-skinned kid, most of the time you don't start the morning thinking about how racism will ruin your day. What you want to know is who will love you, and what surprises that love will bring you that day. It's the world that brings hate to your front door, and it's hate that makes you hide who you are. As a kid, I responded viscerally to "The Bluest Eye," for a number of reasons, starting with the book jacket. Morrison, in the photograph on the back cover, looked like the kind of person my family might have known, and if she was one of us that meant that one of my four beautiful older sisters could, perhaps, write a book, too.

Now I can see that my hope for my sisters was a way of having hope for myself, hope that I might become the artist I wanted to be.

—Hilton Als, "Seeing Things: Toni Morrison's Profound and Unrelenting Vision," *The New Yorker* (February 3, 2020, 68)

Positing in the second-person (you), Als weaves personal reflection into a more traditional analysis of Morrison's work.

Powerful Punctuation

When we study how writers use punctuation with such intention, we learn that these little marks are crafty tools that shape meaning and create certain effects (instead of a series of restrictive rules).

Comma as Zoom Lens

The comma can act like a zoom lens on a camera (Hoffman 1986, 20), giving the reader a closer look at something.

Picture. Zoom. Zoom again.

> They are primeval creatures, bearded and huge, their winter fur peeling off in strips like old wallpaper.
>
> —Hannah Dordhaus, "Prairie Divide," *National Geographic* (February 20, 2020, 74)

Colon as Drumroll

A colon is like a drumroll: it creates a dramatic pause before revealing something you think readers really want to know.

> Our government is helping propel us towards a catastrophe on a scale humankind has never encountered before: the collapse of our life-support systems.
>
> —George Monbiot, "If Defending Life on Earth Is Extremist, We Must Own That Label," *The Guardian* (January 22, 2020)

Asyndeton

Polysyndeton's opposite, asyndeton is the absence of an expected conjunction between parts of a sentence. Writers may choose asyndeton for sound and also precision—conjunctions join and commas separate, a meaningful distinction.

> You pick your piece—a book, an action figure, a frying pan—clicking around to rotate it and find a place for it in the confines of its assigned room.
>
> —Chloi Rad, "Unpacking—Chloi Rad's Most Anticipated Game of 2020," *Gamespot* (December 31, 2019)

Imagine the difference in sound and meaning if the writer had used conjunctions instead.

Items in a Series

Any time a writer has items in a series, there are some real crafting decisions to be made about punctuation. In addition to polysyndeton and asyndeton, writers can also choose periods or no punctuation at all.

Roy's punctuation choices capture the buzz and commotion of a "hostling-jostling" crowd.

> Around them the hostling-jostling crowd.
>   Scurrying hurrying buying selling luggage trundling porter paying children shitting people spitting coming going begging bargaining reservation-checking.
>   Echoing stationsounds.
>   Hawkers selling coffee. Tea.
>   Gaunt children, blond with malnutrition, selling smutty magazines and food they couldn't afford to eat themselves.
>
> —Arundhati Roy, *The God of Small Things* (New York, Random House: 2008, 284)

Sleek Em Dashes

Em dashes—one of our students' favorite techniques—help writers sleekly tuck information into a sentence, layer ideas, and emphasize an image or thought.

> Be warned: We're about to embark on an arduous journey that features math equations, reality questioning, Nazis—hell, there's even a dragon.
>
> —Daniel Chin, "Where Do the Simulations End in 'Westworld'?" *The Ringer* (March 22, 2020)

Layers in some humor!

The
Lookbook

Lookbooks are used in the fashion and design world to show off a new collection so that buyers can get a sense of the style. We can repurpose this concept and invite students to create lookbooks of a single mentor text or the style of an individual author whom they admire. Encourage students to become really curious about the writing with questions like these:

- What are your favorite sentences in this text? Why?
- What craft moves does this writer use over and over again?
- What structural moves stand out to you?
- Find a couple of sentences you'd give a friend to show this writer's style.

As students are developing them, lookbooks can live in a small section in the writer's notebook reserved for this special project. To publish them, students can choose between a DIY or digital option.

Pages from a DIY Lookbook

"Harry Potter and the Poorly-Read Exorcists"

A Margaret Renkl Lookbook

She uses a colon like a small drumroll to introduce a big, important point. It's as though she's slowly, patiently laying out her case for *Harry Potter*.

"Harry Potter and his friends don't exist in real life, but they wrestle with real-life challenges: bullies, rejection, loneliness, fear, grief — and, yes, with clueless adults whose behavior is patently ludicrous."

Because that's what it's truly about: love.

In this article, Renkl's style is like a patiently explaining parent. A patiently explaining parent might think you're ridiculous, but they calmly, gently show you why instead of getting annoyed with you.

Like a parent, she tells stories to help you understand her meaning.

"I was a high-school senior, and my sister was in 6th grade when our mother found a copy of Judy Blume's "Forever" in our shared bedroom. Mrs. Blume's books are frequently challenged, and "Forever" was no exception, featuring a teen protagonist who has sex for the first time. On purpose. With forethought and birth control.

My parents never made any attempt to censor my own reading, but the outcry over "Forever" must have gotten to Mom. Lori was too young, she thought, for a book with a sexually active heroine, and she asked me to downplay its appeal: "She won't listen to me, but she'll listen to you," she told me.

Later that morning, I picked up the well-thumbed book, one my sister had borrowed from a friend. "I heard this isn't a very good book," I said without much conviction.

"It's a great book," my sister said. "I've already read it twice.'"

Pages from a Digital Lookbook

ONLINE RESOURCE 3–4
Directions for Making Lookbooks

chapter four

Learning

ABOUT

Structure

How something
is built

In *The Revision Toolbox*, Georgia Heard (2014) compares the structure of a piece of writing to the construction of a building. Imagine a home under construction that has been framed—the walls are visible and space has been carved out for windows and doors. The rooms aren't complete, but the spaces to be filled have been set aside. That's structure. The spaces where the ideas go.

Let's explore the idea of structure a little now by looking closely at a review written by Glen Weldon, one of our very favorite pop culture critics. As you make notes this time, think specifically about these aspects of structure (which you might study in any text):

- the broad skeletal frame of the text— what comes first, what comes next, and so on
- the parts and pieces that constitute the text
- the movement from one part of the text to the next
- organizational features like paragraphs, chapters, sections, and subheadings.

The Lion King Had the Perfect Villain Song. This Time, "Be Prepared" for Less

by Glen Weldon, *Pop Culture Happy Hour*, NPR (July 17, 2019)

I have seen the new *The Lion King*. *Pop Culture Happy Hour* is devoting a whole show to it this week, so I won't get into a full review here, but just know that, when it comes to one specific aspect of the new film—the one aspect about which I cared most keenly, most deeply, most intensely—the news is not sen*SAAYtional*. It's anything but, in fact.

I refer here to "Be Prepared," the very best song on a soundtrack that does not suffer for good songs. It is the villain Scar's anthem—his pitch to the pack of hyenas to help him effect "the coup of the century."

Here's the original version. Go ahead, click. Treat yourself. Make your day better. Then come back, I'll still be here . . .

[Clip of 1994 "Be Prepared"]

continued on next page

Hi again. So that was pretty great, right? The animation so expressive, so imaginative, so dynamic, so fluid? And the vocal performance, by noted non-singer Jeremy Irons, remains just as show-stopping as ever, for one very specific reason: It's such a pure expression of the character.

Irons' Scar was theatrically sly, performatively unctuous, luxuriously fey. He reveled in his haughtiness, his condescending wit, his sneering contempt for those lesser than he. He not only embraced his status as Other, he wore it like a Bob Mackie gown. He was, in other words, not merely villainous, nor anything so mundane as simply evil. No, he was more fun than that: He was *wicked*.

Now, there's a long cinematic tradition of talk-singing in musical comedies. Rex Harrison and Richard Harris famously barked and yipped their way through *My Fair Lady* and *Camelot*, respectively. It's an effective technique, and Irons could have contented himself to follow in those footsteps. Instead, he chose to impregnate every verse of "Be Prepared" with all the layers of characterization he was bringing to the rest of his performance. You hear it in every lyric— the sly playfulness, the sudden rage, the smug self-satisfaction, the abject delight Scar is taking in his own skullduggery. It's why Irons' "Be Prepared" became, and remains, indelible, even iconic.

Cut to 2019.

The first thing you gotta know is that there were rumors that the new film had cut "Be Prepared" to make room for new (and thus, Oscar-eligible) songs. I, for one, was prepared to storm whatever barricades necessary in protest, and I was not alone. Turns out, they didn't cut it. It's still in the movie . . . sort of.

What they *did* do was cut it down. *Waaaay* down. From nine verses to four, from three minutes to just over one. The new orchestration is almost unrecognizable: Scar's backup hyenas no longer join in with that lusty, insistent "Hummmm / hummmmm / Hummmmm" you feel in your chest—they instead chant "Be prepared / Be prepared / Be prepared" in 4/4 march time; it's what it would sound like if the Boy Scouts imposed

continued on next page

martial law. There's a rejiggered spoken-word intro, to more fully engage the new film's hyenas vs. lions subplot, that turns Scar from a sneering despot spitting vitriol at his subjects ("*Thick* as you are, *pay attention!*") to a mere feckless politician attempting to sway a potential ally ("My vision is clear and wide-ranging / And even encompasses you"). This utter lack of mustache-twirling is a loss—a big one.

[Clip of 2019 "Be Prepared]

And look, I like Chiwetel Ejiofor. He can play a great bad guy—check him out in Joss Whedon's *Serenity* some time, if you haven't. But his Scar is merely, mundanely evil, and his emotional switch just flips from Off to Boiling Rage, while Irons' Scar spent every moment adjusting his dimmer. Musically, non-singer Ejiofor talk-sings his way through the song, only intermittently attempting to hold a note any longer than you'd hold a hot coal.

But the unkindest cut, dear reader? Is that by eliminating all but the very last verse of the original version, the new film's Scar never gets to tell the hyenas—and by extension, us—to "prepare for senSAAYtional news." Sure, maybe he couldn't have put the same English on that legendary line-reading that Irons did (reader, he couldn't have) but it would have been interesting to see him at least try.

Did this all bum you out? I didn't mean to. The new film does have some things to recommend it, which we'll talk about on the show. But my purpose in giving you a heads-up vis-a-vis Scar's anthem was simple: service journalism. Odds are you're gonna see this new *Lion King*, so you should go into it clear-eyed. Manage your expectations. Adjust your parameters.

Be prepared.

VIDEO 4–1
See what we noticed about the structure of Glen Weldon's piece.

ONLINE RESOURCE 4–1
Here you'll find an annotated version of the Weldon text (if you'd like to study our notes on it more closely).

You may be thinking, "That's a lot of decision making about structure to notice and think about," and the truth is, structuring a piece of writing *is* a complex process. When students begin studying authentic writing, one of the first things they notice is that texts are built and organized in a lot of different ways. They don't see conveniently packaged, five-paragraph essays. They don't see a thesis statement neatly stated in the final sentence of paragraph one. What they see is that writers build the frames they need to hold up their ideas. We can study these frames to help students become better writers at the level of structure.

How to Study the Structure of a Mentor Text

If studying craft is about zooming in tight on the text at the word and sentence level, studying structure is slowly panning the camera out, examining the text in chunks. There are two ways you can study structure in a mentor text.

Studying a Specific Structural Element

Sometimes it makes sense to study *specific* structural elements of texts—leads, endings, or transitions. Studying the same key element in different mentor texts gives students vision for crafting that portion of their own texts. Use the same process as for craft study (see Chapter 3), but share just the targeted portion of the mentor texts you've chosen.

> "Teaching is about taking things apart.
> Writing is about putting things together."
>
> —Toni Morrison, from Hilton Als' "Toni Morrison and the Ghosts in the House" (*The New Yorker*, 2003)

Studying a Text's Overall Structure

Many students need support when it comes to structuring and organizing their writing—it's the hardest part. Breaking mentor texts down, paragraph-by-paragraph, helps students see how all the pieces work together and imagine possibilities for shaping their own writing—offering the support they need without resorting to rigid, inauthentic templates or formulas. The typical reading-like-a-writer process is just a little different when studying a text's overall structure:

1 Share a mentor text with students (paper copies or projection).

2 Read the mentor text aloud, paragraph-by-paragraph or in slightly larger chunks of text.

3 At the end of each section, ask students what they notice about the kind of information it contains and then give the section a general name ("This is the background section.").

4 Make a list, in order, of the different sections of the text. You should end up with a map of sorts that reveals how the text moves from beginning to end.

5 Invite students to think about how the structure might inform their writing.

Guiding Questions for Studying Structure

As you teach students how to study a mentor text for structure, you might need a few questions to probe their thinking. After all, many students have never been in an English class before where they've looked closely at the structure of a piece of writing.

What are the parts or pieces of this text?

What does the writer do to begin?

What does the writer do to end?

How does the writer move from one part of the text to the next?

How does the writer divide or chunk the writing?

What elements of this writer's structure might you borrow for your own piece?

Two Tools for Visualizing Structure

You can help students see the structure of a piece by having them arrange it on index cards or cutting up a copy of the text so they can manipulate the chunks.

Index Cards

Your students can play with the structural moves they've just studied using the map they created in the process for studying a text's overall structure. Have them write the name they assigned each section of text on the top of an index card like this.

A: Although we always have mentor texts at the ready, we don't always magically pull out the perfect mentor text. The beauty of conferring with mentor texts is that they offer us great flexibility and endless possibilities. There is always another mentor text to show a path forward for the writer, and we just appreciate the extra confidence they offer us when it comes to helping students who have so many different needs as writers.

This strategy helps students visualize the structure of a mentor text and imagine it as a possible model for their own writing. Students can use the structure cards to jot down ideas. For example, here's what it might look like if a student used the Glen Weldon review to plan their own review of a different song.

Personal Stake Introduction
— The Dixie Chicks is the first country music I ever liked.
— Senior year, new state — connected me to home in a new way.

Defining-the-Review Paragraph
— New music after 14 years! Yay!
— "Gaslighter": nod to what I loved in the past without the heart.

Unpack the Evidence Paragraph
• Military/propaganda motif
• upbeat & harmonious
• bitter without humor

After studying a few mentor texts, students end up with multiple decks of cards representing different structure possibilities, which they can mix and match to explore options for their own writing. Of course, students can also use this activity as a revision tool to map the structure of their *own* draft and clarify their structure.

Scissors

Invite students to grab a pair of scissors and cut apart different sections of a text—their own or a mentor—and then play with the order by moving the pieces around. As they manipulate the structure, ask students to consider these questions:

What are the different ways this text could be put together?	**What are the advantages and disadvantages of each structure?**
Why do you think the writer decided to use the structure you see in the mentor text?	**How do you want to structure your own text?**

GOOD QUESTION!

Q: *How long should a mentor text be in order for students to study structure effectively?*

A: Think about the length that is right for your students— enough to show them the structure at work, but not so much that you lose them. Some articles, like ones in *The New Yorker*, can be twenty or more pages long! In very long texts, structural patterns often appear, and studying just an excerpt will be enough to show students what they need to see.

> **"** ...*no one* knows where to start, and writing is frustration. There are no shortcuts. Students simply need to practice this decision making over and over to get a feel for the complicated zigzag moves writers make to structure a text. **"**
>
> —Liz Prather, *Story Matters* (2019, 103)

Gallery OF Structure Moves

> " If a student is writing an essay but isn't sure how to begin, she can read how other writers have started their writing and try one of their techniques. "
>
> —Georgia Heard,
> *The Revision Toolbox* (2014, 29)

Some conventions of structure are genre specific—a persuasive open letter is structured differently than a persuasive political speech. But other elements of structure apply to every genre. Every piece of writing has a beginning, a middle, and an end. Every piece of writing has to transition between ideas. And sometimes the way a novelist ends a story is the same way a journalist ends an essay.

To really understand an excerpt as part of the *structure* of a text, you need to see how it works with the whole text. Luckily, most of the examples in this gallery are just an easy online search away so you can access the whole text.

Studying structure across genres builds the writer's toolbox, and here we've collected a few structure moves and examples to get you started—either teaching your whole class or supporting students in writing conferences. And remember, you can find all these examples and more in the Online Resources, and the teacher's craftbook provides room to add your own.

Beginnings

To keep the reader reading, so much depends on a good beginning—the lead should propel the reader forward and leave them wanting more. And the beginning, of course, is the first building block of structure.

Drop into a Scene

Opening with a descriptive scene engages the reader's senses and brings them right into the heart of the writing.

The Bachelor is a show designed for happy endings. In the finale of each season, the show's star receives a boulder-sized engagement ring that he hands to one of the beautiful women who has followed him to one of the most beautiful places on earth. They pop champagne and smile and sit down for an interview with Chris Harrison where they smile and look beautiful together.

—Rodger Sherman, "'The Bachelor' Finale Recap: The Wrath of Barb," *The Ringer* (March 11, 2020)

At 6 o'clock in the morning, shortly after the sun spills over the horizon, the city of Kikwit doesn't so much wake up as ignite. Loud music blares from car radios. Shops fly open along the main street. Dust-sprayed jeeps and motorcycles zoom eastward toward the town's bustling markets or westward toward Kinshasa, the Democratic Republic of the Congo's capital city. The air starts to heat up, its molecules vibrating with absorbed energy. So, too, the city.

—Ed Yong, "The Next Plague Is Coming. Is America Ready?" *The Atlantic* (July/August 2018)

Start with the Facts

Opening with facts gives readers needed context for what lies ahead.

In terms of structure, the ending is the other piece (with the beginning) that holds the text together. And since endings linger in the reader's thinking, writers must carefully consider their exits.

Zoom Out

Conclude by zooming out—like a camera panning up, out, and away from the center of action in a movie—to show how the topic matters in a broader context.

> So the question is: What should we, as good people, do about it?
>
> As a male writer, I now make it a point to seek women if, say, I'm looking for experts to interview or I'm listing civil-rights heroes. Maybe that seems awkward and stilted to you, and maybe it is. But here's what I've learned . . . I am a creature of implicit biases.
>
> —Leonard Pitts Jr., "Diversity Matters, Stephen King, but It Doesn't Just Happen out of Good Intentions," *Miami Herald* (January 15, 2020)

> Deer legs are very useful. Their toe bones can be whistles and buckles and fishhooks. The leg bones become knives and flutes. Tendons become glue. I popped the black toes off into boiling water. Slicing with obsidian, I peeled the fur off and then the muscle and tendons. I sawed the ends off the bone. I used a twig to oust the marrow. The carnivore ate it. This would be my flute.
>
> —Nellie Bowles, "How to Prepare for the Complete End of the World," *The New York Times* (March 5, 2020)

The Breakaway Scene

This is the conclusion cousin of the drop-into-a-scene beginning. End by painting a picture that is separate (but related) to the writing that comes before it—leaving a strong, resonant image in the reader's mind.

Have the Last Word

Create an audible finish. The voice behind a powerful, significant quote echoes in the reader's mind.

> He would be able to make clothes that ranged in size from extra-extra-small to extra-extra-large, that people in the Midwest would be able to buy. He would show that ubiquity did not have to mean monotony. It could also be noticeable. "I'm American," he said. "There's no reason this can't work."
>
> —Emily Witt, "Telfar Clemons's Mass Appeal," *The New Yorker* (March 9, 2020)

> The handshake is our national standard for signaling friendship and good intentions to a person you don't know well enough to trust totally. And they're an essential part of a reporter's tool box. . . .
>
> . . . I trade gossip and jokes with beat writers and traveling media, but only after a handshake brings an end to a long winter's separation. Close friends might get a handshake that evolves into a one-armed bro hug.
>
> At this point, shaking hands is as natural as blinking or drawing breath, and in the context of a working journalist's life, it's nearly as common and as useful. That's why it's so hard to stop, even if doing so could save lives.
>
> —Michael Baumann, "The End of the Little Things We Always Take for Granted," *The Ringer* (March 14, 2020)

In prose, structure is built from paragraphs, but studying even a single mentor text will quickly reveal: there's no one way to write a paragraph, there is no required number of sentences, and ideas sometimes extend through several paragraph breaks. Mentor texts dispel the misinformation many students have learned about *the paragraph* and show them the power of *paragraphing* as a tool for rich, complex meaning making.

One Idea in Two or More Paragraphs

Some ideas just can't be contained in a single paragraph, so writers often build a single idea across multiple paragraphs, allowing for more examples, more detail, more nuance.

Single-Sentence Paragraph

Writers love the punch of a supershort, one-sentence paragraph to grab the reader's attention.

Then we caught sight of a nightmare whipped up by the storm: a rain-wrapped wedge tornado half a mile to our right. The chaotic conditions made it difficult for us to keep the monster in sight. Its shape flickered in and out of the rain. We lost our cell phone reception—and all the data we were desperately dependent on for radar apps and communication. We couldn't see beyond 20 feet, and the hail was so loud we had to shout to communicate. Our road was on an intersecting path with the tornado.

—Keith Ladzinski, "Into the Storm," *National Geographic* (February 20, 2020, 26–27)

Endings are sad, but without them, nothing matters.

That was only one of the lessons of the thoughtful, emotional finale of NBC's *The Good Place*, which itself ended after four seasons and only 52 episodes. But, as the show itself stressed in its last couple of installments, heaven is not continuing forever: It's leaving at the right time, when you've done your work. When you're ready.

—Linda Holmes, "A Goodbye to 'The Good Place,'" *Pop Culture Happy Hour*, NPR (January 31, 2020)

Microstory Paragraph

Sometimes one sentence, or a small handful of them, can tell a whole story. Packed with action, microstories speed the pace of the writing.

> I think the question for the NCAA now, as
> March Madness comes in, is: Do we cancel
> games? Do we play them, but not in front
> of a crowd? How do you feel about just this
> phenomenon of playing games with no fans
> in the arena?
>
> —Joel Anderson, Ben Cohen, Stefan Fatsis, and Josh
> Levin, "What the Coronavirus Could Mean for March
> Madness," *Slate* (March 11, 2020)

Idea–Evidence–Explanation Paragraph

In persuasive and argumentative writing in particular (analysis included), writers sometimes follow a familiar paragraphing pattern: present an idea, support that idea with evidence, and then explain the connection between the idea and the evidence.

All-Questions Paragraph

A lot of writing is driven by questions, and sometimes writers make this explicit by crafting a paragraph as a series of questions the rest of the text will explore.

> For another thing, nuclear families in this
> era were much more connected to other
> nuclear families than they are today—
> constituting a "modified extended family,"
> as the sociologist Eugene Litwak calls it,
> "a coalition of nuclear families in a state
> of mutual dependence." Even as late
> as the 1950s, before television and
> air-conditioning had fully caught on,
> people continued to live on one another's
> front porches and were part of one
> another's lives. Friends felt free to
> discipline one another's children.
>
> —David Brooks, "The Nuclear Family Was a
> Mistake," *The Atlantic* (March 2020)

Sum-Up Paragraph

Sometimes a writer needs to get the reader up to speed (quickly and concisely) with some context or background, without getting too far away from their own ideas.

Isabel Allende addresses this bloody period of history in her new novel, *A Long Petal of the Sea*, which traces the exile of a family of Catalonian Republicans as Franco's forces close in on Barcelona. The war offers the Dalmau family and their compatriots no shortage of suffering: typhoid, dehydration, displacement, torture, exile, and death. Unimaginable decisions are repeatedly made out of unimaginable circumstances.

—Sam Buckland, "Love and Solitude in Exile: Isabel Allende's 'A Long Petal of the Sea,'" *The Los Angeles Review of Books* (March 12, 2020)

Transitions

Transitions are the moves writers make from one idea to the next inside a text, often—but not always—delineated by paragraph breaks.

Bridge Words

Sometimes writers carry an important word (or similar word) from the last sentence of one paragraph into the first sentence of the next. We call these bridge words.

Because while spectacular diving catches, nasty double moves, and blazing speed may get more attention, the lifeblood of **the position** rests in the half-second after the ball is snapped.

The late former Steelers wide receivers coaching Darryl Drake spent 15 seasons teaching **the position** in the NFL (and nearly two more decades in college).

—Robert Mays, "The Art of the Perfect Wide Receiver Release," *The Ringer* (January 10, 2020)

The Pivot

In a pivot, a writer complicates an idea by highlighting a contradiction at the beginning of a new paragraph—often using the conjunction *but* or *yet* to join the ideas in a seamless transition.

But the royals are also experts in the exquisite art of revenge dressing—showing up to an event looking like pure fire, in an outfit so stunning and show-stopping, it elicits instant regret from any opposing party. Revenge dressing hinges on looking so good, it hurts anyone who dared to doubt you.

—Michelle Ruiz, "Meghan Markle's U.K. Farewell Tour Is a Master Class in Revenge Dressing," *Vanity Fair* (March 10, 2020)

Continuing Action

Progressive verbs propel the reader forward by creating a sense of ongoing action that spins out of the ideas in the preceding paragraph.

But this is perhaps not the impression you'd get from the initial wallop of *Tragic Kingdom*, featuring one of the decade's fieriest opening four-song runs, all of which were singles: "Spiderwebs," a new-wave rafter-shaker about a girl screening her calls; "Excuse Me Mr.," a dramatic ska-punk number about a girl confronting a dude who's avoiding her; "Just a Girl," a fun-but-menacing-sounding hit about a girl just trying to live; and "Happy Now?", an ever-shifting rock song about a girl chiding her ex. The point was made: *girl* mad.

Following the surge of third-wave feminism in the early '90s, the mid-'90s became the peak of the "angry white female" era in rock and pop.

—Jillian Mapes, "No Doubt: *Tragic Kingdom*," *Pitchfork* (March 15, 2020)

Mentor Texts at Your Fingertips

Some teachers like to haul their computers from desk to desk as they confer with student writers, giving them limitless access to their own mentor-text storehouse, Twitter, and their favorite mentor-text haunts, like NPR and *The Ringer*.

Other teachers create some version of a demonstration notebook (Roberts and Roberts 2016)—a portable, concrete teaching tool where they collect lessons and mentor texts that offer solutions to ubiquitous student writing problems. For instance, if you know that many of your students struggle to find relevant evidence to support a claim, you can dedicate a page in your demonstration notebook to address this problem and take it with you as you confer.

Students who have access to their phones can take a picture of your teaching tool and save it to a writing folder in their phones or print it out and glue it into their writers' notebooks.

ONLINE RESOURCE 4–2
Here you'll find a teacher's craftbook where you can collect your own examples of craft, punctuation, and structure moves to use in your teaching.

A writing issue the strategy addresses.

A strategy to help the writer solve the issue.

A mentor text or two that illustrate the strategy.

Demonstration Notebook Tool for Bridge Words

A space for the student to try the strategy.

chapter five

Learning
ABOUT
Genre

A whole kind
of writing

Genre study is where we put all of our reading-like-a-writer skills together. When we read like writers for genre, we read *across* a set of mentor texts and notice many categories of writerly moves including ideas (*what* writers generally write about in that genre) and also craft and structure (*how* they write about it).

But genre study is important for another reason.

When students leave their formal education, they will still encounter writing tasks they're not quite sure how to approach—perhaps a eulogy, a sales report, a dissertation, a grant proposal, wedding vows. So what will they do? Gather a few examples of that kind of writing—that genre—and study them, of course!

To help you understand this particular form of reading like writer, here are a few examples of short, engaging author bios—the kind you find on the back of your favorite YA novel or on an author's webpage. As you make notes about what you notice this time, be sure to think about what the examples have *in common*. Think especially about length, style, tone, and content (kinds of information). The goal is to understand how to write an engaging author bio.

Jason Reynolds

Long Way Down

(New York: Atheneum, 2017)

Jason Reynolds is crazy. About stories.

He is also tired. Of being around young people who are tired of feeling invisible. So he writes books (a bunch of books) and has even won some awards, but none of them are as important as a young person saying they feel seen. The more that happens, the less tired Jason is.

Kwame Alexander

"Fun, Kid Friendly Bio," Kwame Alexander website

(https://kwamealexander.com/about/me/c/454)

Kwame Alexander has written thirty-five books, three of them in a chair next to a fireplace at his neighborhood Panera Bread. He now writes in a penthouse in London, where he lives. But, he misses the writing studio he built in Virginia a few years ago. It has huge windows, a large painting of John Coltrane, 3,000 books, heated floors, a blue couch, and a loft which was Randy's idea. When he's not writing, Kwame's watching reruns of *The Office* with his soon-to-be six-feet tall middle school daughter, reading manuscripts for Versify, the publishing company he founded, and travelling to schools and libraries across the globe…on Zoom. Kwame has eaten snails, chocolate-covered bugs, and grasscutter, which is like a big rat, which he had no idea he was eating because it was in a really tasty stew he ate in Ghana while building a library and a health clinic in a village called Konko. He's never eaten frogs. But, he has written a book about them called *Surf's Up*. And, some other books you may have heard of, like *The Crossover* and *Swing* and *The Undefeated* and *Becoming Muhammad Ali*, all *New York Times* Bestsellers, which his Dad likes to brag about in grocery stores and doctor's offices. Kwame loves jazz. Kwame loves his family. Kwame loves his job. Kwame's job is to change the world one word at a time. Oh yeah, he also won the Newbery Medal. Whoa!

Tracey Baptiste

The Jumbie

(Chapel Hill, NC: Algonquin Young Readers, 2015)

Tracey Baptiste was born in Trinidad, where she grew up on jumbie stories and fairy tales, and decided to be a writer at the wise old age of three. It took a few more years to get her first publishing contract though. Her debut, a young adult novel titled *Angel's Grace*, was named one of the 100 best books for reading and sharing by New York City librarians. Tracey is a former teacher, textbook editor, ballerina, and amateur librarian who once started up a library in her house in the hope that everyone would bring their books back late and she would be rich! You know, like other librarians. She is now a wife and mom and lives in New Jersey, where she writes and edits books for kids from a very cozy office in her house that is filled with more toys than she can count. *The Jumbies* is her second novel.

VIDEO 5–1
See what we noticed about the genre of short author bios when we looked at these examples.

How to Study Mentor Texts to Learn About Genre

Genre is all about the writer's purpose.

The author crafts a biography to help readers get to know someone.

The memoirist crafts an essay to explore some truth about life.

The critic crafts a review to share their opinion about a new film so readers can make informed decisions about whether to see it.

The conventions of a genre help writers achieve their intended purpose and move their writing out into the world.

When you study *any* genre, you and your students can use the same process to learn what your writing should and shouldn't include, how it should be organized and formatted, and how you might use word choice and conventions to fulfill your purposes. Start by selecting three to five mentor texts in the same genre that show writers tackling different topics and making different choices, and then follow the process for teaching outlined on the following page.

Because you have a cluster of mentor texts to work through, we recommend spreading the reading out over a period of a few days. Think about incorporating some read-aloud (or, if your mentor text is from NPR, listen to the author read it out loud) to bring interest to the reading experience. Here's a system we like:

- *We Go:* Read one mentor text aloud to the whole class and make noticings together.

- *Partners Go:* Have students study the next mentor text in partnerships. Students may still find it helpful to read the text aloud with their partner.

- *You Go:* Have students study the last mentor text on their own, bringing their noticings back to the whole class to share.

> " Writing is learned by imitation. If anyone asked me how I learned to write, I'd say I learned by reading the men and women who were doing the kind of writing I wanted to do and trying to figure out how they did it. "
>
> —William Zinsser, *On Writing Well* (2001, 35)

A Process for Genre Study

Share the Mentor Texts

We like to give our students a stapled packet of all the mentor texts on the first day of a study, but you might also present them one at a time. You can also share the texts digitally on a platform like Google Docs or NowComment.

Make Noticings

Read the mentor texts you have gathered like writers and make noticings about the craft, structure, and ideas of the texts. Students can jot their noticings in the margins, at the bottom of the text, in their notebooks, on group anchor charts—wherever it makes the most sense for how they are accessing them.

Look for Patterns

After a few days, you'll have lots of noticings about the mentor texts that you'll need to gather in one place—either a document you project or a master anchor chart.

Now it's time to think *across* the mentor texts. Look for patterns—what do you see happening again and again? Mark the patterns using colors or symbols. What moves do you see that are unique?

Determine Musts and Mights

If something you noticed appears in every mentor text, place it on the "Must" side of a T-chart—its consistency suggests it is requisite. If something you noticed appears in one or just a few mentor texts, place it on the "Might" side of the chart as a choice a writer might make.

You'll probably find the "Must" column is far shorter than the "Might" column. And that makes sense—every genre has a handful of standard conventions and a large array of individual choices made by each writer.

Turn to Your Own Writing

As soon as we finish a genre study, we plan a flash-draft day and invite students to do some writing in the genre. Often these writing sprints become seeds for longer pieces of writing. At the very least, the exercise allows students to get a feel for the genre, so it's there for them if their ideas ever need to take that form.

The following chart shows a sample "Musts and Mights" chart for author bios.

Musts and Mights of Engaging Author Bios

Must	Might

• Begin with the author's name.
 	
• Write in the third person.
 	
• Include matters of personal pride.
 	
• Be brief (between six and eleven sentences).
 	
• Be filled with the author's own true voice.
	• Use one paragraph or multiple, shorter paragraphs.
	
	• Use phrases like "She is now _____" and "When he's not _____, he's _____" to transition between ideas.
	
	• Use intentional sentence fragments.
	
	• Incorporate humor.
	
	• Include
	  ▸ hobbies
	  ▸ family
	  ▸ favorites
	  ▸ little-known fun facts
	  ▸ titles of books the author has written
	  ▸ awards and honors
	  ▸ where the author was born and/or raised
	  ▸ where the author lives now.

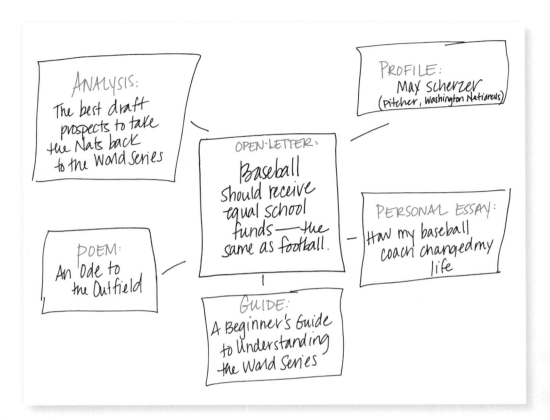

ANALYSIS:
The best draft prospects to take the Nats back to the World Series

PROFILE:
Max Scherzer
(Pitcher, Washington Nationals)

OPEN-LETTER:
Baseball should receive equal school funds—the same as football.

POEM:
An Ode to the Outfield

PERSONAL ESSAY:
How my baseball coach changed my life

GUIDE:
A Beginner's Guide to Understanding the World Series

Consider asking students to choose a piece of writing they have done in the past and identify the genre. Then, ask them to brainstorm how that topic might transform if they wrote about it in a few different genres.

Q: *But what about standards that say I need to teach narrative, informative, and argumentative writing?*

A: To write in any real-world genre (feature article, essay, op-ed, review), students will have to employ these common modes of writing—often more than one in a single piece—to achieve their purposes, just as their mentors do. For example, in the op-ed (argumentative) "Harry Potter and the Poorly-Read Exorcists," *New York Times* writer Margaret Renkl (2019) tells stories (narrative) and presents facts (informative) in order to make her argument about the power of the Harry Potter series. The language of modes helps us name what writers are doing to achieve their purposes, so we *do* teach it—it's essential in almost any genre study!

> ❝My first writing teachers were Beverly Cleary and Judy Blume . . . [the] rich lessons from these two authors helped me develop my own writing chops without a writing workshop or even a writing teacher. I was a student with rich literacy resources.❞
> —Roz Linder, *The Big Book of Details* (2016, 4–5)

Guiding Questions for Studying a Genre

Remember that the key difference when studying a genre is that you are considering what you notice about *multiple* texts.

What types of information does each mentor text include?

Do you notice any special way of laying out a piece of writing in this genre?

What do you think a reader would expect to see in any piece of writing in this genre?

Based on the writing moves you've noticed, what do you think a piece of writing has to have to be considered a part of this genre?

What do most or all of your mentor texts have in common?

What moves have you noticed that happen in only one mentor text?

> "We share mentor texts . . . hoping that their sparkling sentences might lift the writing of our own students, or at least provide scaffolding for them to build sturdier texts of their own."
>
> —Ralph Fletcher,
> *Mentor Author, Mentor Texts* (2011, 4)

Genre Gallery

You can apply the ritual of gathering multiple mentor texts in the same genre, reading them like a writer, and synthesizing patterns to *any* genre you want to learn about with your students.

In this gallery, you'll find genre study possibilities for middle and high school writers. Each section that follows represents a sort of genre study starter kit. Inside each kit you'll find

- what the genre does in this world (its purpose!);
- what it looks like (only the musts, since the specific mentor texts you study, and your expectations as the teacher, will dictate the mights);
- where it lives in the world (our favorite haunts for finding this kind of writing); and
- a short stack (a few excellent mentor texts to get you started—you may need to ramp these up or down depending on your students).

What It Does

Personal essays combine the storytelling of personal narrative with the more formal, worldly writing of essays. Personal essays will often interweave personal accounts with current events or other big topics to shed light on each and draw meaning from the intersection of the two.

Where It Lives

- "Lives" column, *The New York Times Magazine* (1996–2017)
- "Modern Love" section, *The New York Times*
- "Personal Essays" collection, *The New Yorker*
- *This I Believe*, NPR (2005–2009)

What It Looks Like

- Scenes or small moments
- Reflection
- Sensory description
- Past or present tense
- A theme or message
- Transitions between scenes and reflection

A Short Stack

- "This Is Personal," by Stephen Curry, *The Players' Tribune* (August 26, 2018)
- "Confessions of a Synesthete," by Anne P. Beatty, *Salon* (February 16, 2020)
- "My High School Commute," by Colin Jost, *The New Yorker* (March 9, 2020)
- "The Monster of Kings Island," by Christopher Bollen, *The New York Times* (May 2, 2014)
- "How My Korean Immigrant Parents Taught Me to Pursue My Own Version of the American Dream," by Helena Ku Rhee, *Los Angeles Times* (February 28, 2020)
- "Letter of Recommendation: Rags," by Geoff Dyer, *The New York Times* (February 20, 2020)

How-to and Other Guides

What It Does

How-to writing and other guides aim to teach readers something—a skill, a lesson, a new perspective perhaps.

Where It Lives

- "Guides" section, *The New York Times*
- "Tip," *The New York Times Magazine*
- *Life Kit*, NPR (podcast series)
- "Vulture Guides" collection, *Vulture*
- "Guides" section, *The L.A. Times*

What It Looks Like

- A meaningful skill, lesson, or perspective to teach
- Broken-down steps or parts
- Clear, thorough explanations with examples

A Short Stack

- "How to Be a Better Friend," by Tara Parker-Pope, *The New York Times* (n.d.)
- "How to Make the World a Better Place," by Nicholas Kristof, *The New York Times* (n.d.)
- "Homemade Marinara Sauce Is the Fridge Staple You Need at All Times," by Ben Mims, *Los Angeles Times* (March 25, 2020,)
- "What Is Every Song on Taylor Swift's *Lover* Actually About?" by Jill Gutowitz, *Vulture* (August 32, 2019)
- "How to Enjoy Snowflakes," by Malia Wollan, *The New York Times Magazine* (January 7, 2020)
- "The Ringer's 2020 NBA Draft Guide," with scouting reports by Kevin O'Connor, *The Ringer* (n.d.)
- "How to Prepare Now for the End of the World," by Nellie Bowles, *The New York Times* (March 5, 2020)

What It Does

News articles report the who, what, where, when, and why of what's happening in the world. Their primary task is to inform and explain without bias, analysis, or emotion.

Where It Lives

- *The New York Times*
- *The L.A. Times*
- *Newsweek*
- *The Washington Post*
- *The Boston Globe*
- *Time*

What It Looks Like

- The five Ws: who, what, where, when, why
- Sufficient background information or context
- Expert and people-on-the-street quotes
- Clear description

A Short Stack

- "When Will the Tokyo Olympics Be Held? 2021 Game Dates Confirmed," by Dan Cancian, *Newsweek* (March 30, 2020)
- "U.S. Wins Record Fourth World Cup Title," by Andrew Das, *The New York Times* (July 7, 2019)
- "Notre Dame: Massive Fire Ravages Paris Cathedral," BBC News Service, BBC.com (April 16, 2019)
- "There Were (Thankfully) Fewer Alien Enthusiasts Than Authorities Expected. There Were Arrests and a Naruto Runner," by Doug Criss, Christina Maxouris, and Nick Watt, CNN.com (September 20, 2019)

What It Does

Feature articles are like documentaries in words: they zoom in on a relevant, important topic—a person (this is a special type of feature article called a profile), an event, an idea—and uncover the essence of it through interview, research, observation, and analysis.

Where It Lives

- *The New York Times Magazine* and other newspapers and magazines
- *Time*
- *Vanity Fair*
- *National Geographic*
- *The New Yorker*

What It Looks Like

- A *timely* subject
- Descriptive scenes
- Sufficient background information
- Quotations or interview snippets
- Images that add meaning
- Relevant research

A Short Stack

- "How Tierra Whack Is Stepping into Rap Greatness," by Ivie Ani, *Teen Vogue* (March 10, 2020)
- "How Billie Eilish Rode Teenage Weirdness to Stardom," by Jonah Weiner, *The New York Times Magazine* (March 11, 2020)
- "How to Prepare Now for the Complete End of the World," by Nellie Bowles, *The New York Times* (March 5, 2020)
- "'Change Is Closer than We Think': Inside Rep. Alexandria Ocasio-Cortez's Unlikely Rise," by Charlotte Alter, *Time* (March 21, 2019)
- "'Now I Am Speaking to the Whole World.' How Teen Climate Activist Greta Thornberg Got Everyone to Listen," by Suyin Haynes, *Time* (May 16, 2019)

What It Does

The review allows a writer to share their opinion about a product, an experience, or an artifact with other consumers. Reviews can be positive or negative, and writers provide lots of specific evidence to back up their opinions.

Where It Lives

- IGN website (video games and entertainment)
- Restaurant reviews, *The New York Times*
- *The Ringer* (sports, movies, TV)
- *Vulture* (TV, movies, music)
- *A.V. Club* (music, TV, movies, video games)
- *Literary Hub* (literary reviews)

What It Looks Like

- A clear, fresh opinion
- Copious, varied evidence
- Bring-us-into-the-moment-with-you description
- Strong introduction and conclusion

A Short Stack

- *Video Game:* "Reading the Game: The Long Dark," by Jason Sheehan, NPR (May 27, 2018)
- *Music Album:* "Lana Del Rey Crafts a Hypnotic California Sound on 'Norman F****** Rockwell!'" Ken Tucker, *Fresh Air*, NPR (September 6, 2019)
- *Restaurant:* "Peter Luger Used to Sizzle. Now It Sputters," by Pete Wells, *The New York Times* (October 29, 2019)
- *Book:* "In an Enchanted World, Echoes of Today's Political Dramas," by Erin Entrada Kelly, *The New York Times* (March 3, 2020)
- *Movie:* "'Onward' Doesn't Hide the Fact That It's a Tearjerker for Parents," by Rob Harvilla, *The Ringer* (March 6, 2020)
- *Movie:* "'Black Panther' Shakes Up the Marvel Universe," by Manohla Dargis, *The New York Times* (February 6, 2018)

What It Does

Analysis is a piece of writing that explores a text, and a text is anything that has a beginning, a middle, and an end and can be broken down into smaller pieces and examined.

Where It Lives

- *Vulture*
- *A.V. Club*
- *The Ringer*
- *The New York Times*
- *Literary Hub*

What It Looks Like

- Fresh, nuanced claim
- Copious evidence
- Varied evidence (examples, anecdotes, statistics, quotations)
- Thorough explanation of evidence
- Engaging lead
- Strong conclusion

A Short Stack

- "How Ramona Quimby Taught a Generation of Girls to Embrace Brashness," by Rachel Verona Cote, *Literary Hub* (February 24, 2020)
- "The 25 Songs That Matter Right Now," various authors, *The New York Times* (March 7, 2019)
- "Megan Markle's U.K. Farewell Tour Is a Master Class in Revenge-Dressing," by Michelle Ruiz, *Vanity Fair* (March 10, 2020)
- "The Four Greatest 'Tom Brady' Moments of Tom Brady's Patriots Career," by Hank Gilman, *Newsweek* (March 17, 2020)
- "The Women's World Cup Team Is the Most American Thing Out There," by Lauren Peace, *The New York Times* (July 8, 2019)

In our book *Beyond Literary Analysis* (2018), we consider a new definition for analysis and use authentic, real-world analytical writing to teach students how to write smart, fresh, worth-their-time-to-write and worth-your-time-to-read pieces of their own.

What It Does

An open letter is addressed to a specific person but made accessible to readers in the world. It's both personal and public; while intended for its recipient, it has a message that others can benefit or learn from as well.

Where It Lives

- *The New York Times*
- *Teen Vogue*
- *HuffPost*
- *The Players' Tribune*
- Search your local newspaper!

What It Looks Like

- Letter format
- A specific audience
- An opinion
- Copious reasons and evidence to support the opinion
- Personal connection or experience with the topic at hand
- A specific request

A Short Stack

- "A Letter to My Mom," by Jeff Okudah, *The Players' Tribune* (January 2, 2020)
- "A Letter to My Teenage Self," by Solange Knowles, *Teen Vogue* (May 17, 2017)
- "An Open Letter to Mark Zuckerberg," by Aaron Sorkin, *The New York Times* (October 31, 2019)
- "An Open Letter to the NFL Owners," by Kareem Abdul-Jabar, *The Guardian* (July 31, 2018)

What It Does

Letters to the editor "talk back" to a previously published article in that same publication. With a proper greeting and closing, these letters are typically formal in tone but can be just as opinionated and vibrant as op-eds. They can also be more reflective or curious in nature.

Where It Lives

- *The New York Times*
- *The Boston Globe*
- *The Washington Post*
- *The L.A. Times*
- *Newsweek*

What It Looks Like

- Proper greeting ("To the editor:")
- Reference and link to relevant article
- Clearly stated opinion or purpose
- The why: why this topic matters to the writer
- Clear counterarguments
- Strong ending
- Closing (name, city)

A Short Stack

- "Kids Aren't Often Taught by Certified PE Teachers. No Wonder Their Fitness Is Lagging," by Beth Holloway, *The Los Angeles Times* (March 3, 2020)
- "Re: 'Katherine Johnson, 1918-2020: NASA's Shining Star, Undiscovered for Decades,'" by Stephen A. Silver, *The New York Times* (February 25, 2020)
- "Re 'Stop Blaming History for Your All-White, All-Male Movie,' by Aisha Harris (Op-Ed, nytimes.com, Feb. 6)," by Joseph Katz, *The New York Times* (February 22, 2020)
- "Re: 'The Parkland Massacre Isn't an "Anniversary,"'" by Gregory Gibson (Op-Ed, Feb. 14)," by Nadia Farjami, *The New York Times* (February 22, 2020)

What It Does

Poems do the work of every genre—they teach, inform, express, argue, reflect, and analyze—using "the best words in the best order" (Coleridge).

Where It Lives

- Poetry from novels in verse by Jason Reynolds, Elizabeth Acevedo, Kwame Alexander, and Ellen Hopkins
- *Naming the World: A Year of Poems and Lessons*, by Nancie Atwell
- Ted Kooser's "American Life in Poetry," a free weekly column promoting contemporary poetry
- Garrison Keillor's *The Writer's Almanac*, a daily podcast and newsletter of poetry
- TeachLivingPoets website
- Poetry 180 website

What It Looks Like

- Sensory description
- Line breaks
- Theme
- Writing that is crafted with sound in mind

A Short Stack

How could we possibly choose just five? How about some of our favorite poets for studying with middle and high school writers:

- Jason Reynolds
- Kwame Alexander
- Elizabeth Acevedo
- Mary Oliver
- Faith Shearin
- Joyce Sutphen
- Naomi Shihab Nye
- Clint Smith
- Maggie Smith

In his book *Craft and Process Studies*, Matt Glover (2020) shares a whole writing study focused on students choosing and studying their own genres for writing. This is a fantastic way to extend students' genre thinking and provide additional choice.

Bonus Genre Possibilities

The following chart lists some studies that are beyond the scope and sequence of most classic middle and high school curricula but are so interesting and creative that we believe they are worth some real estate in your lesson plan book. Next to each study, we've listed either a specific mentor text or a source featuring many mentor texts.

GENRE	START HERE
Travel	"36 Hours" column, *The New York Times*
Roundtable Writing	"Room for Debate" column, *The New York Times*
Listicle	"10 Things to Do" column, *The L.A. Times*
Satirical News	*The Onion*
Street Portraits & Interviews	*Humans of New York* "Sunday Routine" column, *The New York Times*
Brief History	"The Accidental History of the @ Symbol," by William F. Allman, *Smithsonian Magazine* (September 2012)
Video Scene Analysis	Anatomy of a Scene video series, *The New York Times* Notes on a Scene video series, *Vanity Fair*

GENRE	START HERE
Humor Writing	McSweeney's Internet Tendency (website)
Episodic Memoir	"Five Truths and a Lie About Paxton Avenue," by José Olivarez, *Chicago Magazine* (October 29, 2018)
Process Reflection	"How Taylor Swift Writes a Love Song," by Joe Coscarelli, Alexandra Eaton, Alicia DeSantis, Antonio de Luca, Kaisha Murzamadiyeva, Sasha Portis, and Will Lloyd, *Diary of a Song* video series, *The New York Times* (December 24, 2019)
Oral History	"'Little Women': An Oral History of the 1994 Adaptation," by Ashley Spencer, *The New York Times* (September 12, 2019)
"I Tried _____, and Here's What Happened."	"Learning to Swim Taught Me More than I Bargained For," by Jazmine Hughes, *The New York Times Magazine* (March 24, 2020)
Opinion Mini-Essay	"Soapbox" column, *The Wall Street Journal Magazine*
Authentic Key Passage Analysis	"Close Reads" column, *Vulture*

Teaching with Designed Texts

Designed texts—like the one by Mari Andrew in the following illustration—hold a special place in our hearts and in our notebooks.

The creator of a designed text has made intentional choices about both text and design, and you can study this decision making just as you would study it in a more conventional mentor text. In fact, teaching students to find craft in this parallel context (Ray 2010) can be literally eye-opening for some; students who have trouble noticing the word-, sentence-, and structure-level decisions a writer makes can often "see" design choices, like the ones in Mari Andrew's illustration.

Craft:
Six captions with parallel structure: "[Place]: I grew . . ."

Design:
A loose grid of 3 rows and 3 columns (Can you see it?)

Design:
Three-color palette: brown, purple, green

Craft:
Repetition of the word grew, followed by a concrete or abstract noun

Craft:
Colon after each location

Structure:
Contains six illustrations, each representing a place

Craft:
First person

Structure:
Arrows create a kind of flowchart, transitioning the reader from one place to the next

"Autobiography," by Mari Andrew

Structure:
Moves from small to large: the captions accumulate significance over time

We invite students to study designed mentor texts and then practice making their own, complete with illustrations and captions. After studying "Autobiography," for example, students might create their own designed text about different meaningful places, people, moments, or experiences in their lives. (See the following student example.)

Designed texts also have the potential to offer students a way to structure their more conventional writing. After studying "Autobiography," for example, students might envision possibilities like these:

- a travel essay in six parts
- a memoir in six vignettes, each one about a different place the writer has lived
- an essay that employs anaphora, with the lead of each section a variation of this sentence: In San Francisco, I grew a body.
- a sonnet, with the first six pairs of lines giving an image of each location and the couplet expanding the theme of growth.

Our hands-down favorite writers of designed texts are Mari Andrew (@bymariandrew) and Grant Snider (@grantdraws). We're also big fans of Haley Weaver (@haleydrewthis) and Dani DiPirro (@positivelypresent). For graphic novelists, start with Raina Telgemeier and Jarett J. Krosoczka.

"Designed Text" by Sarah B., Eighth Grade

chapter six

PLANNING

Instruction

with Mentor

suggests
mentor texts
play an
active role

Texts

Teachers use mentor texts in small ways and in large ways—from a ten-minute read-aloud for inspiration to building an entire writing unit.

Teaching with Mentor Texts: A Continuum

Small Investment

Read a mentor text to improve a draft.

Want to make some simple magic happen? After students write a quick draft of their own, show them one mentor text in the same genre. Then, have each writer ask, "What does the mentor text have that my draft doesn't have?" Let these revelations drive revision.

Medium Investment

Use a mentor text to teach a specific skill.

Perhaps you realize that your students would benefit from a lesson on a specific skill—say, effective paragraphing. Consider bringing in the work of a professional. Read the piece together, and then study the way that the writer divides ideas into distinct paragraphs. Your students will be learning this important skill from an authentic source—plus they'll get extra inspiration from reading the words of a pro!

Large Investment

Use a cluster of mentor texts to teach every lesson in your unit.

When you study a few mentor texts in the same genre, you can see myriad writing skills your students will need to become successful writers. Choose the five or six skills they need most right now, then use them to form the backbone of your unit. Each time you teach a writing lesson, pull examples from that same cluster of mentor texts. By the time students have finished their best drafts, they will know these texts like the backs of their hands.

Planning Content

A great piece of writing can teach a writer an almost endless number of skills and techniques. The tricky thing is, there isn't one right lesson or set of lessons to teach with each mentor text, so how do you decide what content is important?

The process we use to determine content for either a single lesson or a whole unit starts with a powerfully written text (or two or three) and some close reading. To help you understand this process, we invite you to go to the Online Resources and find the three mentor texts we've included there for an op-ed study. Print them out if it's easier, or just have them up on a screen as you explore this process with us.

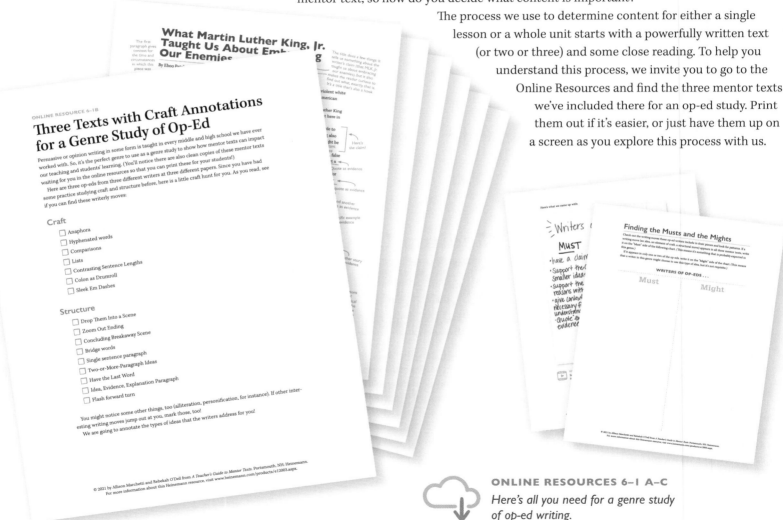

ONLINE RESOURCE 6–1B

Three Texts with Craft Annotations for a Genre Study of Op-Ed

Persuasive or opinion writing in some form is taught in every middle and high school we have ever worked with. So, it's the perfect genre to use as a genre study to show how mentor texts can impact our teaching and students' learning. (You'll notice there are also clean copies of these mentor texts waiting for you in the online resources so that you can print these for your students!)

Here are three op-eds from three different writers at three different papers. Since you have had some practice studying craft and structure before, here is a little craft hunt for you. As you read, see if you can find these writerly moves:

Craft
- ☐ Anaphora
- ☐ Hyphenated words
- ☐ Comparisons
- ☐ Lists
- ☐ Contrasting Sentence Lengths
- ☐ Colon as Drumroll
- ☐ Sleek Em Dashes

Structure
- ☐ Drop Them Into a Scene
- ☐ Zoom Out Ending
- ☐ Concluding Breakaway Scene
- ☐ Bridge words
- ☐ Single sentence paragraph
- ☐ Two-or-More-Paragraph Ideas
- ☐ Have the Last Word
- ☐ Idea, Evidence, Explanation Paragraph
- ☐ Flash forward turn

You might notice some other things, too (alliteration, personification, for instance). If other interesting writing moves jump out at you, mark those, too!

We are going to annotate the types of ideas that the writers address for you!

What Martin Luther King, Jr. Taught Us About Embracing Our Enemies

By Eboo Patel

Finding the Musts and the Mights

Check out the writing moves these op-ed writers include in their pieces and look for patterns. If a writing move (an idea, an element of craft, a structural move) appears in all three mentor texts, write it on the "Must" side of the following chart. (This means it's something that is probably expected in this genre.)

If it appears in only one or two of the op-eds, write it on the "Might" side of the chart. (This means that a writer in this genre might choose to use this type of idea, but it's not requisite.)

WRITERS OF OP-EDS . . .	
Must	Might

Writers [...]
MUST
- have a claim
- support their smaller ideas
- support the reasons with...
- give context necessary f... understan...
- Quote evidence...

ONLINE RESOURCES 6–1 A–C
Here's all you need for a genre study of op-ed writing.

> "Mentor texts enable a teacher, whose planning time and knowledge of every potential genre of writing is limited, to reach every writer in the room, on any given day, whatever the writer needs. Mentor texts enable all of us—teachers and students alike—to do far more than we ever could on our own."
>
> —Allison Marchetti and Rebekah O'Dell, *Writing with Mentors* (2015, 3)

Storing and Organizing Mentor Texts: Three Ideas

Email: If the mentor text is just a sentence or a short passage, paste it directly into the body of an email. If it's longer, paste the link in the email. Write a word or two in the subject line to remind you what you might use this mentor text for (for instance, "review" or "parallel structure"). Send the email to yourself, and when you receive it, move it to a dedicated folder you've created for mentor texts (which could have subfolders).

Custom Twitter Hashtag: Mark potential mentor texts with a hashtag of your own. Our friend Jay Nickerson (@doodlinmunkyboy) started this teacher Twitter trend with his hashtag #NowhereNearMyNotebook. California teacher Jori Krulder (@JoriKrulder) uses #JoriTwitterNotes. Your exact hashtag doesn't matter as much as the ability to type that hashtag into the Twitter search bar later and bring up all the mentor texts you have identified.

Google Drive Folder: Create a free Google Drive folder (our preferred method), and then either copy and paste the mentor text into a document inside the folder or save it as a PDF and drop it inside. You can create subfolders by genre or by writing skill, and Google folders are easy to share with colleagues or with students. Other digital tools like Trello, Evernote, and Padlet also let you store and organize digital content.

Read Like a Writer

Just like our students, the first way teachers approach a mentor text is by reading it like a writer—noticing the writer's moves, giving them friendly names, and theorizing about why the writer might have used them. And, just like our students, we usually end up with a big list of noticings.

Take a few moments now to read through the three op-eds and study the annotations we've included. If you notice craft moves we haven't noted, highlight them and write your own marginal notes. Keep all this handy as you read forward in the process.

Select the Move—or Moves—You Want to Teach

Each thing you've noticed about a mentor text is a potential lesson, so there will be *a lot* of options. You can't possibly teach them all. If you're planning a whole unit, we think five to seven writing skills is just about the perfect number you need, so that means you'll need to narrow your list considerably. Here are some questions to help you do that. As you read through, use them to reflect on the list of op-ed noticings.

Here are the musts and mights we determined for our op-ed study.

> **What foundational skills will my students need to be successful with this genre of writing?**

Every genre has its *musts*, the bottom-line skills that make an op-ed an op-ed or a review a review. Having a beginning, a middle, and an end in a short story. Using rhetorical appeals in an open letter. Finding evidence to support a claim in an editorial. When you look at the writing moves you have noted in a mentor text, ask, "Of these, what does the writer *have* to do to successfully create this kind of text? And what craft *might* the writer want to consider? Do my students know how to do that?"

VIDEO 6–1

See how we made a musts and mights list for our op-ed study.

What are my students ready to learn?

Mentor texts sometimes showcase brilliant writing that your students may just not be ready to replicate—at least without a considerable stretch. Look for next-step skills, writing moves that naturally build on what your students can already do or have recently learned.

Do I see any of these writing moves reflected in my standards or curriculum?

Because the standards you need to teach are based on the skills of proficient writing, you will often see them at work in mentor texts. If you bump these skills to the front of your list, you can teach the required curriculum in the most authentic way possible.

Are there any moves I see writers making over and over again in one or several mentor texts?

If so, take note. You are likely seeing a convention of genre (for instance, giving concise but helpful context in an op-ed) or a common style choice (using punctuation to create voice)—either one a great teaching opportunity.

What would be fun to teach?

When you are required to teach so much, it's important to keep yourself engaged, too. Look for those highlighter-worthy moves that make you say, "I wish my kids would do that in their writing." Try to incorporate at least one fun-to-have craft move in your writing unit.

GOOD QUESTION!

Q: *How do I use mentor texts to teach the skills mandated by my curriculum or standards?*

A: While this planning process is inductive—starting with a mentor text and finding the skills you're going to teach—planning can work the other way, too. Because standards represent the most generalizable of skills, examples of excellent writing in a genre should be able to teach any skill listed in your curriculum framework. Think about this Common Core writing standard, for instance:

CCSS.ELA-LITERACY.W.11-12.1.B Develop claim(s) and counter-claims fairly and thoroughly, supplying the most relevant evidence for each while pointing out the strengths and limitations of both in a manner that anticipates the audience's knowledge level, concerns, values, and possible biases. (CCSSO and NGA Center 2020)

What piece of argument writing could you possibly choose as a mentor text that wouldn't be able to teach students something about claims and counterclaims?

Remembering there is no right lesson or lessons you need to teach, after reflecting on these questions, what could you imagine teaching your own students about op-eds? Think about that first, then have a look at two potential lesson combinations we came up with from those possibilities.

Every lesson in both combinations came from the noticings we made when we read the op-eds like writers.

In both lesson combinations, we are teaching about writing claims, supporting those ideas, and writing a context paragraph because these seem essential to successful writing in the op-ed genre.

Lesson Combination 1

- Using an up-front claim to anchor your writing

- Supporting your ideas with quotes

- Writing a context paragraph

- Using single-sentence paragraphs

- Using anaphora to pack a punch

Lesson combination 1 has fewer lessons and fewer choices . . .

Lesson Combination 2

- Thinking about different ways to write a claim: up-front claim or windup claim

- Supporting your ideas with evidence: quotes, specific examples, and personal experience stories

- Writing a context paragraph

- Crafting drop-into-a-scene beginnings

- Using bridge words to transition

- Using sleek em dashes

. . . than lesson combination 2, which would be appropriate for students who are ready for more options.

ONLINE RESOURCE 6–2
Here is a template to help you plan a whole unit rooted in mentor texts.

VIDEO 6–2
How to Use the Unit Planning Template

Planning Teaching

Once you know *what* you want to teach, you have to decide *how* you are going to teach it. There are three instructional stances you can take while using mentor texts, and the method you choose will depend on your students' experience with reading like writers and your goal(s) for that particular writing lesson or study.

Direct Instruction

With direct instruction, you take the lead and show your students something in the mentor text that you want them to learn how to do. You might choose direct instruction if your students are new to reading like writers or if there is a particular move you know your students need to practice. This method allows you to teach into those needs clearly and effectively, and having a consistent, predictable structure for this teaching streamlines your planning and frees up time for you to spend observing your students, listening to their questions, conferring with them, and giving them feedback. Here's an example of that teaching in action, with an excerpt from one of the op-eds in the Online Resources.

VIDEO 6–3
Teaching Through Direct Instruction

ONLINE RESOURCE 6–3
Here's a template to help you plan a direct instruction lesson with mentor texts.

> *Introduce the writing move students will learn today.*

Today I want to call your attention to how writers use numbers to support an argument. Numbers can speak powerfully to readers, especially when they are surprising in some way. They're more specific, and they also show you've done your homework and know your facts. Look at this sentence from Margaret Renkl's piece about efforts to ban Harry Potter books:

> *Elaborate on why the writer might choose this move.*

> Little surprise, then, that two decades of efforts to protect children from imaginary spells have made no difference at all. Harry Potter titles have sold more than <u>500 million copies worldwide</u>.

> *Show students examples in the mentor texts.*

If she had just said something like, "Sales of Harry Potter titles have been phenomenal," it wouldn't pack quite the same punch. The number is more credible, especially with the hyperlink so you can check it out yourself.

As you go back to your drafts, reread with an eye for numbers. Is there anywhere you've said something generally that, with a little research, you could actually quantify and say more specifically?

> *Invite students to try the work of the lesson in their own writing.*

VIDEO 6–4
Teaching Through Modeling

Modeling

While the teacher also leads in modeling, it's less formal and direct. Modeling is a bit like letting students peer inside your brain as you read like a writer. With a mentor text either projected or in everyone's hands, you think out loud as you notice:

> "So, I'm noticing here that the author _____, and I'm thinking one reason he might have chosen to do this is _____. But another thing I'm wondering about is _____, and this reminds me _____. What do you think?"

You might choose modeling if your students need to refresh their reading-like-a-writer skills or if you want to walk them through a lengthy passage, pointing out several craft moves along the way.

> "We lead students to generalize the conventions of a genre to all forms of writing. We connect the thinking in one writing unit to the next— showing how in each unit writers repeat the same moves, no matter what they are composing."
>
> —Kelly Gallagher and Penny Kittle, *180 Days* (2018, 85)

Inquiry

In inquiry-based instruction, you and your students work together, sharing responsibility for noticing and naming craft. Successful inquiry work is built upon a foundation of strong direct instruction and modeling. Students need ample opportunities to observe their teacher and try on their own thinking to gain the confidence and tools needed to answer the open-ended question "What do you notice?"

When we pull sentences or texts for an inquiry-based craft study, we might have a particular teaching point in mind, or we might just want to give our students an opportunity to build their reading-like-a-writer muscles. We recommend you use inquiry as often as you can. When teachers encourage students to name what they notice separate from any teacher agenda and bring the craft that allures them back to their own work, they write from a place of agency and enthusiasm.

VIDEO 6–5
Teaching Through Inquiry

Blended Teaching

Direct instruction, modeling, inquiry. The most effective teaching blends all three of these methods. In inquiry work, for example, there might be a moment where it makes sense to jump in and offer students some help to name what they see so they can think more deeply about a craft move. Or, during direct instruction, it might make sense to open up the conversation to students with some general questions to help them make connections: *Have you seen this craft move before? Where? Can you imagine a place in your own work where it might help?*

Different Ways to Teach with Mentor Texts

- *Whole Class:* Teach writing moves that are essential to your writing unit or to your curriculum.
- *Small Group:* Teach writing moves that apply only to a small number of students' writing, writing skills that need fixing up and extra support, or writing skills that nudge your most advanced writers forward.
- *Individual:* Teach writing moves that come up as you talk to students one-on-one about their individual pieces of writing. These moves help students address specific problems in their work or help elevate their writing.

chapter seven

ASSESSING

Students'

WORK WITH Mentor

Texts

Using a mentor text to improve writing is pretty simple: students read the mentor text, they notice what the writer is doing, and they try it themselves. But let's be honest: it's not always *easy*. This isn't a one-size-fits-all model—no good teaching is.

When you assess students' work with mentor texts, you will see that students in the same class are in a variety of different places in their understanding and application. Why the range of development? Well, consider this:

Every writer in your class has a unique history with writing and unique needs.

Like any skill you teach, some students will catch on to reading like a writer faster than others (who may need more intensive practice).

By the time they reach middle or high school, many students have had their writing red-penned past the point of recognition, and they've been filled with warnings about the rights and wrongs of writing. This history makes it hard for some students to engage with the play and experimentation that comes with mentor-text study.

We are asking students to strive to write at the same level as the professional writers they are studying, and this is a big ask (but it's one that we can help students reach toward through supportive practice).

Many students also arrive with rigid thinking because they've been given formulas for writing for so long and never really considered that a writer has choices. These habits are strong and take time to unlearn.

Student Work with Mentor Texts: A Continuum

Although students' needs will differ, there are predictable reflections of what Carl Anderson (2018) calls students' "partial understandings" of reading like a writer. While our goal is to move students toward independence, each place along the continuum is a spot where mentor texts can help students do more as writers.

	BEGINNING	IMITATING	MOVE LIFTING	TRANSFERRING	CRAFTING INDEPENDENTLY
INDICATORS	Students have trouble making meaningful noticings in a mentor text and may struggle to notice and name anything at all.	Students are extremely reliant on the mentor text as though it were a formula or fill-in-the-blanks worksheet. They are not yet able to generalize craft moves.	Students are able to search for writing moves in a mentor text and choose to apply some of them to support their own writing in increasingly authentic ways.	Students purposefully access a repertoire of writing moves they've learned *across* different texts and choose what works best for their current writing.	Students have internalized the process of reading like a writer—it's unconscious and automatic. They pull from a growing toolbox of writing moves whenever they write.
WHAT THE STUDENT MAY BE THINKING	"I know I'm supposed to notice something in this mentor text and try it in my own writing, but I have no idea how."	"If I follow this writer's exact moves in the exact order, I will end up with a good piece of writing."	"I need to carefully find the writer's moves in this mentor text so that I can make my own writing stronger."	"I can use things I've noticed in mentor texts in the past to benefit my writing now."	"I know how to strengthen any piece of writing I create by employing the tools I have learned."

	BEGINNING	IMITATING	MOVE LIFTING	TRANSFERRING	CRAFTING INDEPENDENTLY
CHARACTERISTICS OF STUDENT WRITING	There's no evidence the student has tried any crafting moves, or the student has tried them, but they don't really work.	Student uses the mentor's ideas, structures, and even phrasing almost exactly. Writing has the mentor's voice, not the student's.	Writing shows the student using craft moves directly from a mentor text to strengthen their own ideas and authentic voice.	The student's voice is strong in writing that is intentionally crafted, but the influence of specific mentor texts is becoming less obvious.	The piece reads like any good writing—exhibiting a powerful combination of both conscious and unconscious crafting decisions that serve the writer's intentions.
BUILDING ON PARTIAL UNDERSTANDINGS	Support students in individual writing conferences and with scaffolding activities like those in the Online Resources.	Teach students to generalize writers' moves using phrases like these: • Writers of narratives zoom in to give detail to the most important part of the story. • Writers who want to create rhythm in their writing use repetition.	Because reading like a writer is more mechanical than intuitive for these students, encourage them to use a craft glossary to see how their learning is transferable or to set mentor text based writing goals.	To help students become even more intuitive as they read like writers and internalize the process, encourage them to read a mentor text first without a pencil in hand and then go back and quickly circle the top five moves they noticed.	Just have students keep reading and writing!

To help you understand student work along this continuum, consider the difference in how two students applied what they learned after studying this sentence in Paula Hawkins' *The Girl on the Train* (New York: Riverhead Books, 2015):

I know this house by heart. I know every brick, I know the colour of the curtains in the upstairs bedroom (beige, with a dark-blue print), I know that the paint is peeling off the bathroom window frame and that there are four tiles missing from a section of the roof on the right-hand side. (Hawkins 2015, 18)

The first student is imitating Hawkins' craft moves fairly directly:

I know this pool by heart. I know every tile, I know the slipperiest spot on the deck (below the stands, in front of the gutters), I know that the blocks tremble every time you step up to start and that the sunlight blinds you only when you reach the second yellow marker.

—Norah P.

Another student innovates on Hawkins' passage and makes it her own:

I'm not very good at video games, but I know this one by heart. Each monster and how to kill it. Every corner of the map (From the south western deserts to the barren tundras nestled in the mountains). I've talked to every NPC and seen the dialogue to our one-sided conversations dozens of times. I know which flowers and fish to catch and harvest and which power boosts they give my character and the ways I could cook it. It is all just pixels, but it always feels like there is something new to explore.

—Molly G.

For some writers, staying closer to the mentor text enables them to take risks and embrace new writing techniques, while more confident writers use the mentor text more as a launching pad. Let students try on the mentor's moves at the level they feel comfortable with, but be sure to make time for them to share. Often, hearing a student spin off in a new direction will inspire other students to try something new next time.

> "When we are first learning to study the craft of writing, we are very intentional in our reading like writers. We try to read like writers on purpose. And when we return to our own drafts, we often draft and craft on purpose in a particular way that we have come to know from our study. . . . We choose to do on purpose certain things with our writing that we trust will, over time and with experience, become far more automatic for us as we draft."
>
> —Katie Wood Ray,
> *Wondrous Words* (1999, 62)

GOOD QUESTION!

Q: *What do I do if students don't think they need to use mentor texts to lift the level of their writing?*

A: In our classes, it's typically our most confident writers who sometimes think this. Here's how we open the door to more mentor-text inspiration:

- Remind students that this is what anyone wanting to learn to do a task better does—watches an expert in the field and tries to mirror what they do.
- There is no piece of writing that couldn't be made one percent better. Ask students if they think the mentor text might give them just one idea to make their pieces one percent better.
- Zoom in close when you study, and encourage students to find small moves to use. Some writers mistakenly think their writing needs to look just like the mentor text when they are finished.
- In writing, we often don't know whether or not something will work until we try it. Writers who give a move a try can be surprised to see it really works and makes their writing better.
- Let students make final decisions, even if they don't lead to the strongest writing. The whole point of mentor-text study is to teach students that writers make choices.

Quick Tools for Assessment

How will you know where each student is on that continuum as you move through the year? Well, you can look at students' mentor-text annotations, ask them about their decisions in writing conferences, and read their writing, but this all takes a lot of time. To save some of that time, here are a few quick, go-to tools you can use to check in on students' progress throughout the writing process.

Mentor Move Conference

Have a quick, ninety-second conference focused solely on mentor-text work. Ask students to show you and talk about one craft move they have annotated in a mentor text and then tried in their own writing. A minute of talk will speak volumes about how much students are understanding in their mentor-text work.

Mentor Move Exit Ticket

In lieu of conferences, you can ask students to submit one mentor-text annotation or one example of them using a mentor-text noticing in their own writing. You can have students do this on an index card as an exit ticket or fill out a quick Google form.

Collaborative Annotation

Print a sentence study in a large font, split students into teams, and have each team annotate the sentence for craft, style, and grammar. While teams share what they marked, you can notice which teams are on track and which might need more support.

Padlet Wall

A Padlet wall of student writing gives a bird's-eye view of who easily applies the noticings from a mentor text and who doesn't yet. After teaching a lesson rooted in a mentor text, ask students to try it immediately so you can quickly triage any issues or partial understandings that may arise.

Revision Talk

At the end of class, after students have chosen a strategic place to revise their writing using something they gleaned from a mentor text, use a simple turn-and-talk to give partners a chance to explain the changes they made and how they improved the writing. Do a little bit of discreet eavesdropping as you circle the room.

Draft Highlighting

When you are ready to look at drafts or final products, it can be hard to intuit where writers have tried mentor-text moves, so ask students to highlight or underline them and then add comments to explain crafting decisions.

Tracking and Self-Assessment

Students can keep a chart in their notebooks (or digitally) to track what they are trying and assess how it is working in their writing. A quick peek will show you what students are trying and where they might need support.

Mentor Text Self-Assessment Chart

WRITING MOVE FROM THE MENTOR TEXT	HOW I USED IT IN MY WRITING	HOW MUCH THIS HELPED ME		
		THIS HELPED ME A LITTLE	THIS HELPED ME SOME	THIS HELPED ME A LOT!
Acknowledge the other side and disagree.	I acknowledged that people think that school should start earlier because students need time for sports after school, and then I discussed why I disagreed.		X	
Use video as evidence.	I incorporated a TED Talk by Wendy Troxel called "Why School Should Start Later for Teens."			X
Use medium–medium–small paragraph structure.	I used this throughout my whole draft.			X

Building Independence Through Transfer: The Craft Glossary

The ultimate goal of mentor-text work is independence, of course. We want students to amass a huge toolbox of writing moves that they can grow over time as they read new texts and apply in a wide range of writing contexts throughout their lives.

It helps to make this goal explicit, and one way to do that is to make the metaphorical toolbox an actual thing—we call it a craft glossary.

A craft glossary is a collection of writerly moves from mentor texts, examples, and a catalog of places the student has experimented with each move. The glossary—which students will return to again and again for ideas and inspiration—can live either in an online document that students add to as they study mentor texts or in the back of a notebook.

Excerpt from Sam's Craft Glossary

WRITER'S MOVE	EXAMPLE FROM MENTOR TEXT	WHERE I'VE USED IT IN MY WRITING
Example-adding dash	"That's too bad because being a good listener can help you in every aspect of your life—with family and friends and with your colleagues at work." "How to Be a Better Listener," by Adam Bryant, *The New York Times* (March 4, 2019)	• Notebook time on Sept. 10 • How-to Guide • In my How-to Guide reflection in my notebook
Fast-paced writing (lots of periods)	"The halls surged with a parade of beautiful strangers. They laughed too loud. Flirted. Shrieked. Raced. They kissed. Shoved. Tripped. Shouted. Posed. Chased. Flaunted. Taunted. Galloped. Sang." *The Impossible Knife of Memory*, by Laurie Halse Anderson (New York, Speak: 2015)	• Notebook time on Nov. 4 • Independent writing on Nov. 5 • Notebook time on Dec. 6

continued on next page

WRITER'S MOVE	EXAMPLE FROM MENTOR TEXT	WHERE I'VE USED IT IN MY WRITING
Compound sentences to join two or more ideas	"American Dream may be selling experiences, but the mall always *was* an experience." "Welcome to the Era of the Post-Shopping Mall," by Amanda Hess, *The New York Times* (December 27, 2019)	• Notebook time Jan. 6 • How-to Guide • Open Letter (WW2) • Independent writing on Nov. 4 • Independent writing on Nov.18 • And many many more times

After studying a mentor text (a sentence, a whole text, a group of texts), from all the many possibilities, each student chooses just a move or two to add to their glossary. The moves should be ones they admire and want to practice in their own writing. When they use the writing move, they add the place where they practiced it—both small attempts in their notebooks and larger attempts in polished pieces of writing.

When students lift writing moves out of an isolated mentor-text study and into a new space, it helps them generalize the moves so they can be useful in all different kinds of writing. A craft glossary also helps students become increasingly metacognitive about their work with mentor texts—planning for what they want to try and reflecting on their decision making.

References

Als, Hilton. 2003. "Toni Morrison and the Ghosts in the House." *The New Yorker*. October 20, 2003. https://www.newyorker.com/magazine/2003/10/27/ghosts-in-the-house.

Anderson, Carl. 2018. *A Teacher's Guide to Writing Conferences, Grades K–8*. Portsmouth, NH: Heinemann.

_____. 2000. *How's It Going? A Practical Guide to Conferring with Student Writers*. Portsmouth, NH: Heinemann.

Atwell, Nancie. 2014. *In the Middle: A Lifetime of Learning About Writing, Reading, and Adolescents*. 3rd edition. Portsmouth, NH: Heinemann.

Beers, Kylene, and Robert Probst. 2015. *Reading Nonfiction: Notice and Note Stances, Signposts, and Strategies*. Portsmouth, NH: Heinemann.

Council of Chief State School Officers (CCSSO) and the National Governors Association Center for Best Practices (NGA Center). 2020. "CCSS.ELA-LITERACY.W.11-12.1.B." www.corestandards.org/ELA-Literacy/W/11-12/1/b/.

Crystal, David. 2012. *The Story of English in 100 Words*. New York: St. Martin's.

Fletcher, Ralph. 2003. *A Writer's Notebook: Unlocking the Writer Within You*. New York: Harper Collins.

_____. 2011. *Mentor Author, Mentor Texts: Short Texts, Craft Notes, and Practical Classroom Uses*. Portsmouth, NH: Heinemann.

Gallagher, Kelly. 2006. *Teaching Adolescent Writers*. Portsmouth, NH: Stenhouse.

Gallagher, Kelly, and Penny Kittle. 2018. *180 Days: Two Teachers and the Quest to Engage and Empower Adolescents*. Portsmouth, NH: Heinemann.

Glover, Matt. 2020. *Craft and Process Studies: Units That Provide Writers with Choice of Genre*. Portsmouth, NH: Heinemann.

Heard, Georgia. 2014. *The Revision Toolbox: Teaching Techniques That Work*. Portsmouth, NH: Heinemann.

Hoffman, Gary. 1986. *Writeful*. Location: Verve Press. Quoted in Harry R. Noden. 2011. *Image Grammar: Teaching Grammar as Part of the Writing Process*. Portsmouth, NH: Heinemann.

Kittle, Penny. 2008. *Write Beside Them: Risk, Voice, and Clarity in High School Writing*. Portsmouth, NH: Heinemann.

Linder, Rozlyn. 2016. *The Big Book of Details: 46 Moves for Teaching Writers to Elaborate*. Portsmouth, NH: Heinemann.

Marchetti, Allison, and Rebekah O'Dell. 2015. *Writing with Mentors: How to Reach Every Writer in the Room Using Current, Engaging Mentor Texts.* Portsmouth, NH: Heinemann.

———. 2018. *Beyond Literary Analysis: Teaching Students to Write with Passion and Authority About Any Text.* Portsmouth, NH: Heinemann.

Noden, Harry. 2011. *Image Grammar: Teaching Grammar as Part of the Writing Process.* Portsmouth, NH: Heinemann.

Prather, Liz. 2019. *Story Matters: Teaching Teens to Use the Tools of Narrative to Argue and Inform.* Portsmouth, NH: Heinemann.

Prose, Francine. 2007. *Reading Like a Writer: A Guide for People Who Love Books and for Those Who Want to Write Them.* New York: Harper Perennial.

Proulx, Annie. 2020. "Annie Proulx: Quotes: Quotable Quote." Goodreads. www.goodreads.com/quotes/172515-you-should-write-because-you-love-the-shape-of-stories.

Ray, Katie Wood. 1999. *Wondrous Words: Writers and Writing in the Elementary Classroom.* Urbana, IL: National Council of Teachers of English.

———. 2010. *In Pictures and in Words: Teaching the Qualities of Good Writing Through Illustration Study.* Portsmouth, NH: Heinemann.

Reynolds, Jason. 2018. Interview by Trevor Noah on *The Daily Show with Trevor Noah.* Directed by Paul Pennolino. Aired January 23 on Comedy Central.

Rief, Linda. 2007. *Inside the Writer's-Reader's Notebook.* Portsmouth, NH: Heinemann.

Roberts, Kate, and Maggie Beattie Roberts. 2016. *DIY Literacy: Teaching Tools for Differentiation, Rigor, and Independence.* Portsmouth, NH: Heinemann.

Smith, Frank. 1987. *Joining the Literacy Club: Further Essays into Education.* Portsmouth, NH: Heinemann.

Stockman, Angela. 2015. *Make Writing: 5 Teaching Strategies That Turn Writer's Workshop into a Maker's Space.* Highland Heights, Ohio: Times 10 Publications.

———. 2018. Hacking the Writing Workshop: Redesign with Making in Mind. Highland Heights, Ohio: Times 10 Publications.

———. 2020. "Confronting Print Barriers in the Writing Workshop and Leveraging Loose Parts." March 22, 2019. http://www.angelastockman.com/blog/2019/03/22/using-loose-parts-to-scale-print-barriers-in-the-writing-workshop/. Accessed April 27, 2020.

Teacher's College Reading and Writing Project. 2014. "Research Base Underlying the Teachers College Reading and Writing Workshop's Approach to Literacy Instruction." https://readingandwritingproject.org/about/research-base.

Woodson, Jacqueline. 2014. "Jacqueline Woodson on Growing Up, Coming Out and Saying Hi to Strangers." Interview by Terry Gross on *Fresh Air.* Aired December 10 on NPR. www.npr.org/blogs/codeswitch/2014/12/10/369736205/jacqueline-woodson-on-growing-up-coming-out-and-saying-hi-to-strangers.

Zinsser, William. 2001. *On Writing Well: The Classic Guide to Writing Nonfiction.* New York: Harper Collins.

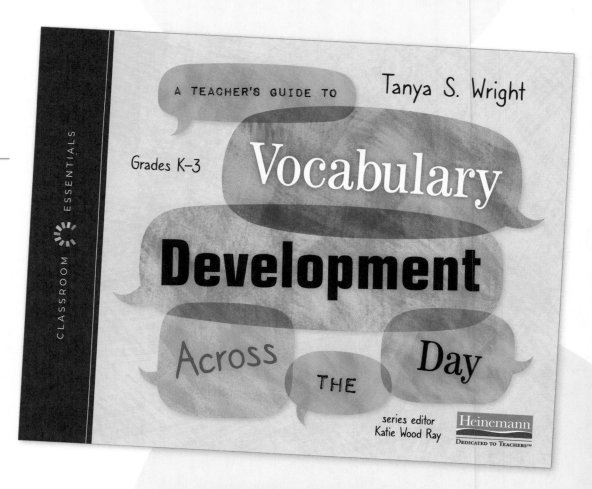
A TEACHER'S GUIDE TO

Vocabulary Development Across the Day

By Tanya S. Wright

Young children love to learn and use new words; the key is to tap into their natural curiosity and excitement. Tanya Wright shows you how to create opportunities for children to think about and use words in meaningful contexts during read-aloud, content-area learning, reading instruction, and writing instruction—all day long! Classroom videos of teachers and children learning about words bring the ideas to life, and a friendly, accessible "What We Know" feature highlights important research that informs the practice.

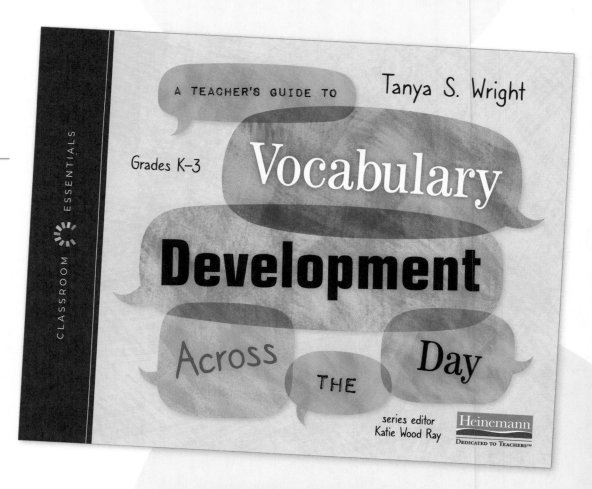

Grades K–3 / 978-0-325-11277-0 / $19.50

A TEACHER'S GUIDE TO

Writing Workshop Essentials:
Time, Choice, Response

*By Katherine Bomer
and Corinne Arens*

Katherine Bomer and Corinne Arens introduce teachers to the rituals and routines of writing workshop and suggest ways to take small, incremental steps toward implementing them. Shared from the viewpoint of two veteran educators who understand the issues and obstacles teachers face day-to-day, *A Teacher's Guide to Writing Workshop Essentials* also serves as a refresher for experienced workshop teachers looking for a chance to refocus, clarify, and extend the work in their practice.

Grades K–5 / 978-0-325-09972-9 / $19.50

A TEACHER'S GUIDE TO
Reading Conferences

By Jennifer Serravallo

"Conferring," writes Jennifer Serravallo, "is where the magic happens." In this foundational guide to reading conferences, she reveals that this seeming magic is actually purposeful, responsive instruction. Jen presents the moves and language that can be used in conferences for six specific instructional situations: assessing, goal-setting, strategy lessons, and more. Classroom videos, note-taking forms, and suggestions for connecting emergent bilingual learners' language goals to reading goals provide tools and support to help you get started with reading conferences.

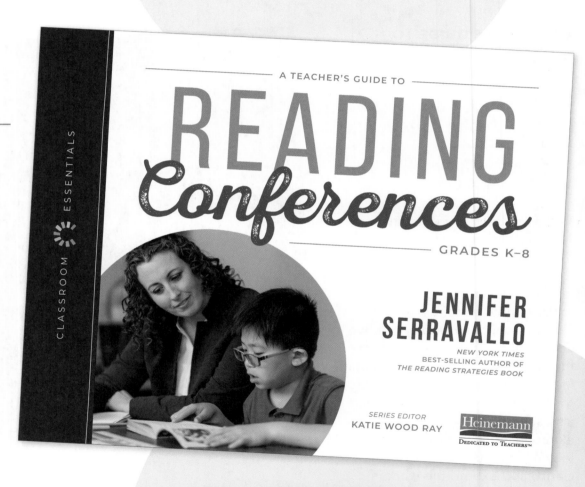

Grades K–8 / 978-0-325-09915-6 / $19.50